EVERYBODY HAS TO
CRY SOMETIME

To: MARGARET e
HUGH

Everybody Has to Cry Sometime

J Kenneth Rodgers

Best Wishes,
J. Kenneth Rodgers.
(Kenny).
3/9/08

UPFRONT PUBLISHING
LEICESTERSHIRE

Everybody Has To Cry Sometime
Copyright © Kenneth Rodgers 2004

ISBN 1-84426-302-9

First published 2004 by
UPFRONT PUBLISHING LTD
Leicestershire

Printed by Copytech UK Ltd

Acknowledgements

I would like to thank all those who have been instrumental in converting dreams (and some nightmares) to the reality of this book.

NANCY – Without whom dreams would be for dreaming and not living.

JEANETTE – Without whom the book would still be in my fair handwriting rather than a typed manuscript.

JOHN AND TRISHA – Without whom I would not have had the confidence to attempt to go to print.

UPFRONT PUBLISHING – Without whom there are memories but no book.

THE 'MARY TINTIES' – (the married-intos/the in-laws) – Duncan, Jessie, Alistair, Jimmy, Linda, Andy and Wee Elaine without whom there is no partnership in marriage.

MUM, DAD, LILIAN, JIM, MARLENE, ELAINE, BOBBY, YVONNE, DAVID, COLIN, AVRIL and GRAHAM without whom there is no family.

Dedicated to the future:

Gary, Greg, Joanne, Gavin, Shona, Roddy, Lorna, Alisdair, Bobby, Claire, Lilian, Jim, Lorraine, Kevin, Paul, Stephen, Jim, Iain, Aiden, Vhairi, and Mikayla and all their kids.

CONTENTS

CHAPTER ONE

Who are you for a Rodgers?

'The Family' was already bigger than average, as my Mum and Dad had provided me with three big sisters and two big brothers before I bawled my way into this world on 6th January 1957. Lilian, Jim, Marlene, Elaine and Bobby were already filling nappies and charging through their infancy and early childhood. We were not rich and famous, but we all had at least double-barrelled names – Christian names, that is.

Lilian was therefore Lilian Davidson;

Jim – James Allan;

Marlene – Marlene Anne;

Elaine – Elaine Elizabeth;

Bobby – Robert Leslie;

and me, John Kenneth.

My Mum liked proper names and I suppose it was a sign of respect for existing or previous members from both sides of the family. Names were handed down like good clothes; they could even coincide with some great event or be borrowed from some highly respected person outwith the family.

Names, like times, also change and hand-me-down names, like clothes, become unfashionable. Old, 'respectable' names have been eclipsed by the new media, sports and pop personalities. This has bred a clutch of Kylies, Charlenes, Dannies, Brads, Mels, Romeos and the likes.

In the fifties and sixties, forenames might have given you a sense of who some of your relatives were, but it was your surname which marked out your potential character and standing in the community. The cry was, *'Who are you for a Rodgers?'*

I didn't know then, but I know now that for Rodgers we were the product of the soil and hard toil. There was no blue blood, no knights and no nouveau riche to ease the rigours of the earlier centuries. The occupations of our ancestors confirmed we were 'ordinary common folk'.

On my Dad's side, we stretched back to Arthur Curragh, a farm labourer in Ireland, whose son, William, emigrated to Scotland during the mid-1800s (like thousands of others who left the Emerald Isle in face of the potato famine). The Curraghs, from around Auchinleck, and the Rodgers, from Cumnock, formed my father's side of the family, allied to the Watts and the Hardies, who originated from Aberdeenshire.

On my mother's side, the alliances centred around the Allans from Larkhall and the Davidsons from Hamilton. Basically, we were three parts Scottish and one part Irish, with an American strain 'thrown out' for good measure, and now living in Wyoming and beyond.

There were no exotic job titles then and in the main, our male ancestry consisted of farm labourers, coal miners, furnace labourers, iron miners, wood forester, gas man, labourer, dairyman and crofters. Our place in the social strata of the day was really borne out by the registered occupations of our female ancestors – they were variously described as general servant, domestic servant, housekeeper, estate worker, domestic nurse, domestic servant (cook), dairymaid, housekeeper and cotton weaver.

The most 'upmarket' occupations in our ancestry included a cinder molter (presumably part of the iron industry), a silk weaver around 1881 and a caustic soda maker in 1923. Various 'scholars' are also listed but the curiosity 'value' lies in our past association with the Murrays, who were described as 'bank agents', and in particular, Bentley Murray (c1870), who appeared not to have a job, but had 'income derived from dividends'. The 'dividends', if they existed, were never passed on to the Allans or Rodgers – instead we inherited a work ethic and a sense of pride in being able to work and make it (whatever 'it' was) on our own merits.

In more recent times, I never knew my Mum's mum, but my grandpa was John Allan, *aka* Wee Jock. Big families were pretty much the norm back then and my Mum had three brothers, John, Tom and Willie, and three sisters, Margaret, Molly and Annie. The brothers were all characters in their own right and Margaret, Molly and Annie were quiet and loving sisters.

The real character in my Mum's family, apart from my Mum, was undoubtedly 'Wee Jock', a miner from Lanarkshire. In his later years, he frequently came to visit us from his home in Low Waters, Hamilton. He liked the peace and quiet of the Darvel countryside and would often arrive at weekends dressed in a dark tweed-style suit with a pipe and matches in the right-hand jacket pocket and chunks of cheese in the left. I never really understood the chunks of cheese in his left pocket, but when he and my Dad would return from the pub after a few pints and 'haufs', the cheese was gone! He was always up bright and early the next day with no sign of a hangover. I don't think Wee Jock ever visited Spain, but I suppose the cheese was the equivalent of 'tapas' in the pocket.

Loudoun Hill is situated about a mile to the east of Darvel, on the old A71 road to Edinburgh. It is a 'volcanic plug' and history has it as the site of a Roman fort. It is also reputed to have been the site of numerous battles, including those fought by our 'Braveheart', William Wallace, Robert the Bruce and the Covenanters.

It transpires that Wee Jock had seen a few battle sites himself and was a veteran of World War I. He had served in his 'local' Regiment, the Cameronians (Scottish Rifles), whose HQ was at 129 Muir Street, Hamilton.

In the Great War, the Regiment served in France, Flanders, Macedonia, Egypt and Palestine, and the 7th Battalion was the last to evacuate Gallipoli.

Having survived the Battle of the Somme and the Great War, Wee Jock became a miner in Lanarkshire. The miners rows were out of town and meant an eight mile walk for mum, as a young girl, to the school in Low Quarter, Hamilton. Serving and surviving two World Wars did not save the Cameronians from a review of Regiments and Wee Jock proudly attended the disbanding of the Cameronians on 14 May 1968. After 279 years of wartime exploits, a peacetime military review achieved what wartime enemies couldn't – they killed off the Cameronians.

None of my grandpa's wartime exploits came from him, nor my Mum and Dad. They emerged from a chance meeting with a local worthy at the top of Loudoun Hill, who asked the inevitable, 'Who are you for a Rodgers?'

Even after retiring from the pits, Wee Jock took up a job as a night watchman. Late at night or early morning calls usually meant bad news and I remember the early morning call on 4 April 1973, when my Mum was told he had been found dying in a cabin, 'defending' the steelworks.

Not to be outdone in the family size front, my Dad had four brothers – Jim, Peter, David and William, and two sisters – Rhoda and Annie.

Jimmy and Ina were my grandparents on my Dad's side and I can remember visiting them on a couple of occasions at Saltcoats. Jimmy grew tomatoes and had 'budgies'. The tomatoes were not just any tomatoes – they were yellow, just like some of his budgies. Yellow tomatoes in the 1960s were a bit like gay men – you didn't see a lot of them, but when you did, they stood out a mile. This of course was in the days when the mention of 'gay' did not mean you were homophobic.

Jimmy, like 'Wee Jock', was a real character. In his late teens and early twenties, he had gone to America and worked as a 'hired hand' moving from farm to farm to secure work. His wanderlust ended when he returned to Scotland after the First World War and married Williamina Watt-Hardy – thankfully, Ina for short. He retired to his budgies and yellow tomatoes after completing his job as a foreman with Shell Mex. Apart from his sojourns to America, his other claim to fame was as a follower of junior football club, Saltcoats

Victoria for over forty years – he must have been a patient man!

We were therefore ordinary people with no hidden fortunes, but equally, there were no shady dealings, debts or abject poverty. Times were hard, but seemed happy with no real sense of sadness or grief, which develops with age and through time, friendship and love.

Like many kids, I don't have a vivid recollection of my earliest real memories. The first three or four years of life I suppose are like Alzheimer's in reverse – you build up the brain power and strength to progressively learn and remember things, as opposed to losing your brain power and forgetting things. In short, I don't really remember anything until after we moved to Darvel in 1959.

Darvel is a small town in East Ayrshire, in South West Scotland, with about 3,000 inhabitants. It is the most easterly of the three 'Irvine Valley' towns of Galston, Newmilns and Darvel, all of which straddle the River Irvine as it meanders its way to the sea on the Ayrshire coast.

It's a pretty anonymous town, with probably three main claims to fame. It is the birthplace of Sir Alexander Fleming, who discovered penicillin; Sammy Cox, the Rangers and Scotland footballer, hailed from Darvel; and up until the arrival of foreign imports and cheaper overseas labour in the late 1980s/early 1990s, it had a thriving lace and textile manufacturing industry, which rivalled that of Nottingham in England.

Anonymous or not, there was an inherent sense of pride in Darvel (or at least, in Darvel of old), as recalled by local resident, Val McKay (age 96):

Dear Sir
Did you know that at one time Darvel had an outdoor curling club? It was situated in an old stone building at the top of what we called the 'Pond Brae', a continuation of Jamieson Road. It had two ponds, one for curling and one for skating. We

had no world champions but the pleasure and competition was there for both curlers and skaters. Darvel also had a quoiting club which had a senior and junior Scottish champion among its members. There were three tennis clubs in Darvel at one time, one of which, Darvel Gowanbank, held the Singles and Doubles Championships of Ayrshire. The other two were in Priestland. We also had a nine hole golf course at Loudounhill where the sand quarry is now. There was a Darvel burgh band which competed with the best bands in England and eventually won the British Band Championship at Crystal Palace. There was even a Boys' Brigade Pipe Band.

John Campbell, a keen athlete and manager of the Darvel branch of the Clydesdale Bank, was responsible for starting the Darvel Athletic Club. We had over 20 members at the start. The club house was the one handed over by the curling club and was a bit primitive. It had an outside shower we used after training. Tuesday and Thursday were training nights but on Saturday some of us competed in local sports and actually won prizes. One member went further afield and won at Powder Hall.

Sadly these features of Darvel life of the 1920s and 1930s are all away now – the curling club owing to the vagaries of the Scottish weather and the rest just due to lack of interest.

Incidentally, the John Campbell mentioned became Sir John for services rendered and signed his name on all Clydesdale Bank notes after he became Chairman of the Clydesdale Bank. [*]

Pride in the past, however, does not necessarily relate to faith in the future of Darvel or any town or city. The past can be fondly remembered, but not lived in.

People remember insults and compliments in about equal measure and that is why my first real memory of the past is of being wheeled down the street in a big, black pram by my

[*] Source – Autumn 2002 issue of the Valley Advertiser

sister, Lilian. Elderly residents would peer into the pram and would regularly remark, 'Oh she's a lovely wee lassie with her blonde, curly hair.' I think it was then I decided to get a haircut and walk more!

My first wee sister came along in 1959 and she was, and is, the inimitable Yvonne – Yvonne Lorraine Margaret to be precise. No TV then, but my Mum and Dad still managed to conjure up a sensual-sounding French name with my Aunt Margaret.

My Mum and Dad were, and are, a real double-act and with over fifty years of marriage, they are a real polished double-act.

Mum is the most practical, honest, caring and beautiful person. Mrs Baxter hasn't a look-in when it comes to making soup, as Mum is the best in the world. She cares so much for the family that it hurts. She would like to take any pain and hurt suffered by her children and shoulder them. She would have your cold, flu, your broken bones, your tears and grief and what do you get in return? A real mum without comparison. In stereotypical terms Mum was the gatherer; she gathered money, friends, love and affection and the whole family.

This intense caring meant that family setbacks and incidents, which other parents would regard as fairly trivial in the scale of things, were a serious source of concern to Mum.

Dad was the hunter, the provider, the comedian, a shooter and a fisher. He was also a piper and, as part of the Ardrossan & Saltcoats and then Darvel Pipe Bands, he played at Marymass in Irvine, gala days and Burns' Suppers. He couldn't read music, but he mastered playing the pipes and we would often fall asleep to the skirl of the bagpipes and in his most modern phase, this included a wee tune by the Pipes & Drums of the Royal Scots Dragoon Guards, 'Amazing Grace', and also Paul McCartney and Wings' 'Mull of Kintyre'. A dab hand at darts, he and Sam Dunlop were the double-handed champions of Ayrshire in their day.

In her early teens, my Mum 'went into service' with the Dean family. She was a housemaid and surrogate mother all rolled into one in the home of the Deans, where she stayed for five years. It's an association and affection which continues to this day, through visits and cards to celebrate birthdays and anniversaries, the most recent of which was the now Mrs Brownlie's ninety-second birthday, on 31 October 2004.

In 1996, Mrs Brownlie exclaimed, in the story of her life:

'I was left, at 32, after nine wonderfully happy years, with Ian who was six months old, and Margaret just four. Dr Steel immediately brought me Lily, our wonderful Lily, who at 16 nursed the baby as her own and stayed with us daily for almost five years. She spoiled everyone, including me! She went on to have ten (actually eleven) children of her own, and is as wonderful today as ever, living happily with her husband Robert, in Darvel, with two middle-aged sons who see no reason to leave home!!! And I'm not surprised!'

Beyond that period of 'domestic service' my Mum has always been a mum whom you could neither pay by the hour, or for the love, care and affection she produces.

After an early spell as a fireman, my Dad became a Council worker. Following a bout of suspected TB, the outdoor work helped to improve his health and fitness. Periods of work with the Councils in Ardrossan and Saltcoats, Dreghorn and Springside, were followed by the longest posting to Darvel in Kilmarnock & Loudoun/East Ayrshire. Loyalty and enjoyment of his job meant an accumulation of over forty years service with 'the Council' by the time my Dad retired.

These were the backgrounds of the characters whose world's collided, resulting in marriage in 1948, at the age of twenty-four, and who remain the 'matriarch' and 'patriarch' to the family.

Both Mum and Dad have worked like 'Trojans' all their lives and really did embrace the old work ethic. Both agreed 'there would be *"nothing on tick"* in this house'. The 'Store

Quarter' was a wee bit of an exception, but even then, everything was paid at the end of the quarter. Our Co-operative Dividend number was originally 902 and when business and customer numbers were booming, the number changed to 3902. Boom turned to bust for the Co-operative shops in Darvel and now all but the fruit shop, which masquerades as a Ladbrokes 'betting shop', have succumbed to the wooden-window syndrome – they've been 'boarded up.'

Before the advent of Asdas, Morrisons, Safeway, Sainsburys and Tesco, Darvel and many a Scottish town had its Co-op (store) Bakers, Butchers, Fruit Shop, Hardware and Drapery; separate shops but co-operatives. The socialist roots of the Co-operative movement couldn't halt the movement out of town and out of fashion until the late 1990s. It's ironic that many of the major 'multiples' now offer what the Co-op offered in its heyday – the Co-op 'van' or store-boy delivered your orders to the door. Yesterday's 'van' has been replaced by order on-line via the superhighway. With more in-store value and community values, the Co-op is making a comeback – a comeback that's too late to save the sandstone buildings that once proudly proclaimed, *'Darvel Industrial Co-operative Society Limited – Instituted 1840.'*

Economics were pretty simple back then and without the aid of Keynesian or Monetarist Theories, my Mum and Dad worked out that if we couldn't afford it, we didn't have it, and yet we didn't really want for anything. Most families were the same, with the exception of the 'upwardly mobile' and the 'never works, never wants' brigade.

In season, pheasants, partridge, ducks, pigeons, rabbits, hare and trout were all in plentiful supply, as Dad was a good shot and fisher. After teaching us to fish in the local 'burns', the River Irvine and the Glen, we progressed to the Avon at Drumclog and the Clyde as it flows through the Clyde Valley in Lanarkshire. We grew potatoes, turnips, carrots, Brussels, cabbages and peas and although we were never anything like self-sufficient, it all helped. For relatively poor people, we had a 'rich man's diet', but we never reached the stage of saying, 'Aw, no pheasant again!'

'Hillcrest', Manse Brae, Darvel – otherwise known as the new cemetery, was where we stayed and sat in 'perfect peace and isolation', above the rest of the town. My Dad was the Cemetery Superintendent, or 'gravedigger' as the folks in Darvel would have it. In his early days as the new 'gravedigger', my Dad was in one of those, 'Who are you for a Rodgers?' conversations with a couple of old biddies down the street, when the topic came round to good bones to make soup. My Dad's offer to get them 'some good bones' for soup was hastily rejected when the 'who are you for a Rodgers?' question was answered by, 'I'm the new gravedigger.'

My uncles and aunts used to love coming to visit us in Darvel. There was Jim and Dot in the Ford Consul, Duncan and Annie in the Ford Anglia, Rhoda and Barclay, William and Mary, Tom and John on the bus, and Willie 'six-guns' and his entire family on the motor bike and side car – it seems there were a lot of cowboys in East Kilbride where Uncle 'William' stayed!

In the absence of money and before the advent of the people carrier, my Mum and Dad never owned a car, so it was Shanks' pony for us. It was something we never queried – we didn't have a car and we didn't need one – we were 'visited' not 'visitors'.

Visits and weekend stays by Aunt Annie and Uncle (big) Duncan meant the girls, Marlene, Elaine and Yvonne vacated their room for the bed settee in the living room. The settee folded down to a double bed and we had plenty of bed linen but on occasion blankets could be a problem especially in winter; so it was that the grey and the black coats would emerge from the press opposite the pantry in the kitchen. These muckle great coats were the eiderdowns of their day.

Complete with my curly blond locks, it came time to go to the primary school – the 'wee school'. This involved a two mile return journey each day which, even then I realised would be a real chore for my Mum to do day in and day out, especially with Yvonne and Davy (David Gordon) now on the scene. By the second day at school, I boldly declared my independence, and from now on, my Mum needn't accompany me to and from school each day.

Some kids cried on their first days at school, but this was short-lived, and the race was on to see who would be the next world racing driving champion by running round the school buildings at playtime. Would it be Jim Clark? Stirling Moss (*Aka* Stoory), Beefy? Edgar? Kerr or Wee Kenny?

Halloween was usually a good time at the primary, as there was a party with games and dookin' for apples. My head was in the pail filled with water as I bit into the biggest apple of the lot – success! Chuffed with myself, I gorged it down and an hour or so later, made my independent way up the road to 'Hillcrest'. By the time I reached John Aird's lace factory at Glen Brig, my stomach was doing 'wheelies'. I would hold it in until I came to the wooded area at Manse Brae (well, bears shit in woods, and there were doken leaves to wipe my bum). The best laid plans of a wee Ayrshire boy went aft aglay with the first squirt of diarrhoea, followed by a 'meltdown' which escaped from my pants and made a lava flow down my legs and below my short trousers. Independent or what?

The final ignominy was sitting in the sink getting washed and explaining to Mum that, although her wee boy could walk up the dangerous road himself, he couldn't control his bowels.

Christmas was also usually a good time at the primary (a party, pantomime or play, but no big soor apples to induce involuntary shiting). So it was that the P4 Nativity Play got under way, 'choreographed' by Miss McFarlane and Mrs Smith. Sitting (yes, **sitting**) cross-legged on the wooden floor, I was suddenly aware that things had 'stopped' and I was being beckoned to join the 'cast' backstage. One of the Wise Men had taken appendicitis and I had been called off the 'subs' bench' to present myrrh to Mary and Joseph for the baby

Jesus. It was over in a flash and I think I fluffed my lines, all six words.

There is and was something ironic about being born on Epiphany and my role in the Nativity Play. My Mum had always stressed I had been born on Epiphany but, to me, that was the day that Christmas decorations came down and we returned to school after the holidays, rather than the day the Wise Men from the East reached Jesus in Bethlehem.

These 'happy days' were not tainted with sadness or grief or any sense of being poor. Even pain was a short, sharp sensation which didn't last, but which is literally etched on my head.

The rocking horse at the big park was a source of great fun and fascination to a boy of five. Curious as to how it worked, I ventured closer and closer as the horse was rocked on its axis by some older kids. The higher it went, the closer I got, and the more I learned about how it worked. Until - wallop! Blood was streaming from my head through my blond hair. A hurried visit to the doctors and the split head was mended but the rocking horse was no longer a winner for me. Off came the curly blond locks of hair, which had been matted with blood.

Darvel once boasted its very own Roxy Picture House (cinema), which stood next to Paterson's, later Struther's fruit shop. The picture house showed its last western in the early sixties. (I don't think it was 'Gone with the Wind'). But as one picture house door closed, another opened, as we used to sneak into the building which was a haven for playing in when it was wet and cold (and it was frequently wet and cold in Darvel). The rows of chairs and curtains and ropes all provided a stage for us to play on. That was, until we emerged from the dark recesses under the stage with our nostrils full of the smell of shite. Someone had been caught short, and emptied his or her bowels under the stage. The empty Darvel picture house became out of bounds, but there was still the 'flea pit' or Rex in Newmilns (which was demolished in 2002), that was if the Darvel crew were brave enough to enter into 'Apache territory'. Whilst Glasgow and bigger Scottish cities had a 'gang culture' in the 1960s and 1970s, smaller Scottish towns had 'town rivalries' which, whilst not acute, could still merit a 'doing' if you were in the wrong place at the wrong time.

The Junior Secondary was the next step on the educational ladder. Unfortunately, there were also a few snakes at the 'big school' and snakes had to be confronted or avoided. Avoidance was not my strong point, then or now, but I wasn't town-wise, never mind street-wise. In Scotland, the smaller you are, the harder you have to try and prove you're 'big'. 'Wee man' can be a term of endearment or an insult and a challenge to be 'big'. Who says it, and how it is said, is critical. A fight here and a fight there soon established the wee man's credibility, to the point where I became the Henry Kissinger of my year. I got in more trouble stopping or preventing fights than I did from being in them. It wasn't really a case of me being really 'hard', and more that other kids (with fewer brothers and sisters) got fed up fighting the Rodgers family, as the first flurry of fists was followed by a declaration of *'If you beat him you'll have to fight me next…., and me next…., and me next,'* by Bobby, Marlene and Elaine.

From the 'splendid isolation' of Hillcrest, school offered a collective and competitive challenge, or at least, that's how I rationalise my approach looking back. I was a country boy playing catch-up with the kids from the town, who already knew and had played with each other. School was an opportunity to learn and develop and get involved in new activities; it was a time to shape yourself and your future, or so it seemed to me. While other kids 'plunked' the school, I reckoned if I've got to be here, I'm going to give it my best shot. There were others more gifted and talented that me, but I got 'stuck in', and the reward was attendance at the annual prize-giving ceremony, to collect certificates of merit and excellence and books in recognition of being in the first three of the class. Ironically, apart from a passing glance, these books were never read and like many of yesterday's mementos, have been packed and stacked in the attic.

School was more than books and lessons, there were games and sports. Sport was also a real passion for me and Recreation Park, the home of the mighty-but-skint Darvel Juniors was the scene of my first game of 'organised' football for the school. Mrs Young took the team and it was rumoured that if you left your y-fronts on under your shorts, she came into the dressing room and personally removed them. We crushed Crossroads 8-0 and we were all real Scotsmen under our shorts! Football really was the national sport then and we played morning, noon and night on the public parks with our jumpers down for makeshift goals. The rivalry between the top of the town – myself, my brother Bobby, Jim Browning, Ricky McNaughton, Munger, Jack Collins and Cat Houston (funnily enough he wasn't a goalkeeper) – and the bottom of the town – Beefy (who went on to play in goal for Motherwell – I suppose someone has to do it?!), Stoory, Dung, Grimley and Sammy Cox (grandson of the legendary Rangers and Scotland player, Sammy Cox) – was reflected in various clashes at Kate Ross', down by the big park. These were fraught affairs, which usually ended in a fracas or fight; sometimes me and Bobby as 'brothers-in-arms', and sometimes involving me and him as 'brothers-in-battle', especially when I scored an own goal to give the bottom of the town victory. This was pre-Bosman days and the fixture fizzled out as players moved house and loyalties and friendships got mixed/blurred or maybe, just maybe, we got older and acquired other interests.

Up until the early 1960s, the family revolved around those brothers and sisters in front of me. By the time I had arrived at the 'wee school' all the others had gone to the 'big school' and by the time I reached the 'big school' my siblings had already left or were about to leave. There was a sense of chasing my brothers and sisters and never quite catching up with them and at the same time, not knowing if I really wanted to catch up with where they were going or what they were doing. As brothers and sisters in the country life and pursuits followed the seasons – fishing in the spring and summer; swimming in the river when it was really warm was popular and would be followed by building a fire and cooking potatoes on a stick in the warm embers until they were brown and burnt on the outside and white and fluffy in the middle. Occasionally, a can of beans on metal plates was the added ingredient and recipe for a full days outing. Late summer and autumn could involve helping out by lifting bales of straw and picking potatoes at local farms before a period of winter inactivity and near hibernation indoors in front of a coal fire. No central heating, no 'Game Boys', no computers and no mobiles – only each other for company and a laugh.

'Doing the shoes' became a rite of passage and by the time I was twelve it was my turn. Initially this was no problem as it was a bit of a chore but it was just cleaning and polishing the school shoes with the old Cherry Blossom or Kiwi polish. As the years progressed 'doing the shoes' became a decidedly dodgy business after Jim became a baker and Bobby a butcher. The ridges on the soles of Jim's shoes became filled with dough and the occasional raisin and worst still was the sawdust and bits of mince in the tread of Bobby's shoes. These foot odours came from well-respected trades and are nothing to compare with the dogs' shit that fouls its way into every groove in modern day shoes and trainers. Life certainly didn't smell of roses in the 1960s but dog shit was not the curse of every pavement in every town.

Rural life was not idyllic but it did have its idiosyncrasies. 'In the coal house we had "dross and brickets" to back up and fuel the fire and in amongst the black diamonds we had potato skins, potato skins!'

'The goodness of the potato lies directly beneath the skin,' my Mum would chant, but we had some thick skinned potatoes and their role in life became the back up to the dross and brickets in the Raeburn stove. Nowadays they would be loaded for loaded restaurateurs to fuel our hunger and turn the noble tattie's outer skin to a delicacy.

With farms all around us we could live off the land; we could get 'double yokers' from Dunlop's farm. These were very large eggs and the equivalent of the poor wee brown hen expecting twins – they had two yokes. For thrupence a week (one pence) we would take our turns to deliver the eggs, double wrapped in brown paper bags to the Flannigan sisters in Green Street, Ethil and Margaret. Their names were old and their living room reflected a clean dullness that was decidedly pre 1960s. The visits and the double yokers became more infrequent as age and standardisation caught up with the sisters and the brown hen respectively.

Strang's farm was more modern; it was a piggery. Huge pigs in pens the equivalent of battery hens in cages stuck out their snouts to devour whatever was in the trough. Piglets ran to suckling mothers in families of eight, nine and even ten in blissful ignorance of their fate and destiny with the plate.

The adult pig was caught and strung up at Strang's farm ready for the killing. Dad shot it and the farmer slashed it from throat to groin and its entrails spilled on to the clean concrete for Jim to clear up. We had pork for a week and spare ribs before they ever became fashionable and, therefore, by definition, expensive for what you were actually getting.

The rhythm of rural life was interspersed by the lure of the town. Playing the bagpipes and playing darts were Dad's passions. The brown pay-packet was handed over to my Mum every Friday and in return for his toils my Dad got a brown and bronze 'ten bob note '(fifty pence). Gowanbank Hotel or the Black Bull Inn were the places to sharpen his skills with the arrows and his wit. In good weeks this might extend to another ten bob note for a pint on Saturday and the Monday night league game. Mum always gathered the brown pay packets and dealt out the money. It is a skill that is practiced weekly and comes as second nature except on one Christmas when inexplicably the empty brown pay packet remained in Mum's hand and the green pound notes sparked to life on the red hot coals on the open fire. Only a few green backs were retrieved from the fire as in despair Mum's fingers burned.

For youths going down the town, it meant playing football, 'Newmarket'; going a 'plunder' or experimenting with smoking – cigarettes for the inhalers and cinnamon sticks for those with asbestos lungs.

In summer nights 'Newmarket' was common; it was a hundred yard run over the front hedges of the gardens in Paterson Terrace. If that was a lung-buster, so too was running away from the aftermath on a failed plunder on local fruit trees and strawberry plants. Even more of a lung-buster was the smoking or failed attempts at smoking. Getting a 'single' (fag) and a match was a major coup; smoking it was the *coup d'etat* but failing that a cinnamon stick could be bought and lit leaving your credibility still intact. Still intact of course until you took the first intake of smoke from the hollow stick and realised you were breathing fire – you were smoking a fuckin' fire lighter and no bugger warned you! There was no notice on the packet and you had just tried to inhale raw flames and look cool – yeah right!

On the more solitary side there was little to beat fishing. At Hillcrest the grass cuttings from the regular cutting of the cemetery plots were piled at the four corners of the cemetery. The bottom left hand corner was the favoured spot for digging worms for fishing. Not just any worms; these were bramble worms with their distinctive whitish yellow rings around reddish bodies. These were much more attractive than dew worms; at least they were to the fish. These worms were perfect for catching brown trout on the rivers Avon, Glen and Irvine, but not as perfect as a 'raspberry'.

The raspberry does not feature in the classic fishing guides as bait for brown trout but it can be effective when you're in a jam, so to speak. The River Irvine was fishing well in early August and, with a little run on the water from a fresh shower, I set off in search of a few brownies with my treasured bramble worms in a ' jeely jar'. They would do the trick or at least they might have done if they had not slipped from my pocket to freely feed the fish waiting downstream. All was lost with lost worms and I made my way up to the small bridge at Priestland – to walk home wormless and fishless – that is until I spied some ripe raspberries on the other side of the river and decided to have a feed. After six or eight raspberries the thought crossed my mind that the small, conical inside of the ripe raspberries looked to me like a small white grub, which the fish would eat. How would they look to the fish? Let's try and see.

Under the shade of the bridge I put the master plan to the test with two raspberries masquerading as grubs on the end of a size twelve hook. Two casts later and the big fish was hooked on raspberries. Playing a one-pound trout on an eight-foot rod under a six-foot bridge gave the fish a fair chance, but with a wee bit of luck and invention and the big fellow was landed, sweet as you like.

Moving from fish to family we were 'close in adversity' and would rally against the world, but we were not and are not the most expressive in terms of our affection for each other. The closeness of brotherly and sisterly relationships was set by age and sex differentials. We were brothers and sisters but probably didn't fully realise the value of blood ties in the face of friendships which were formed outside the family. But in the 1960s, we were all young with little or no real sense of who we were as individuals, let alone in our relationships and values as a family.

We were not rich and famous, but we were a happy lot with a Mum and Dad who provided and cared for us. There were the occasional fall-outs, rows and a few 'skelps' here and there, but we knew a 'skelp' (or a belt) from Dad was for our own good or we deserved it – that was normal to us. When we, five or six brothers and sisters, had caused a 'rammy', the trick was not to be top of the heap but bottom of the heap, as this left less of you to be 'skelped'. The cry was *that was your fault* as calm and order was restored by Dad.

We didn't have a lot, but we had the love and support of Mum and Dad and nowadays, these seem to be exceptional traits, as 'star' after 'rising star' or 'falling star' seem to have managed it to 'the top' through and despite having parents from Hell. Still, I suppose some of these 'revelations' are true and I suppose some of these things sell books. Genuine abuse is as hard to comprehend and abhorrent as is abuse of the genuine.

Wiliam Watt: My Great, Great Grandfather in a Abraham
Lincoln statesman-like pose.

Top: Top: 'Wee Jock' (Bottom Left) preparing for The Great War
Bottom: Loudoun Hill, a volcanic plug to the east of Darvel

Left: Dad aged 5
Right: Dad 'the piper'

Mum and Dad – married on 31st March 1948

CHAPTER TWO
Friends, Football, Flares and France

Newmilns, like every Scottish town, has its 'character families', and in this case, it was the home of the Ferries, the Gilmours, the Kilties, the Spences and Johnnie 'Borrie'. These 'characters' and 'character families' were not 'families from Hell', but individuals and families with 'old-fashioned' character. Character could be a trait, talent or skill, which had come to characterise an individual or even the whole family. They were 'lovable rogues', 'rough diamonds', or simply 'gallus' – they had a bit of spirit, a sense of humour and a bit of get up and go about them – they were not 'beige people' who melted into life's canvas; they were upfront and admired, even if grudgingly admired. A lot of these characters still frequent the Valley, a bit greyer with age but still more colourful than their counterparts of yesteryear, and still holding the attention of the younger generation who recognise the story, if not the true character of the individual.

In 1969, the Newmilns Secondary School became home of the senior school pupils from Darvel. Junior Secondary Schools were on the way out and through consolidation and amalgamation of school rolls, new academies spawned. The Newmilns School has long since been demolished (and is now the home of the dry ski slope), but when it was there I encountered – 'Wee Eck' (Alex Wallace), the history teacher. The pipe-smoking Wee Eck was well regarded, but nevertheless, prone to some Mickey-taking, including being locked out of his own class.

His entrance after one such lock-out was like a scene from Aladdin – huge puffs of 'chalk-dust' filled the air, or so it appeared, until the cry went up,

'Sir, your pocket's on fire.'

He never again forced the door with his Swan Vestas matches in his jacket pocket, but he kept the same jacket, complete with leather patch over the 'smoking' pocket.

The big family became the biggest family in Darvel as, after Yvonne, Davy (David Gordon), Colin (Colin Cameron), Avril (Avril Allison Ogilvy), and finally, Graham (Graham Stewart Anderson) came along. We were then thirteen, including Mum and Dad – a football team plus two subs. I was slap-bang in the middle, with three elder sisters and two elder brothers, two younger sisters and three younger brothers. At the peak of our numbers at Hillcrest, the boys' room had a double bed, a single bed and two bunk beds, in order to sleep all six brothers. The girls' room was slightly less crowded (as Lilian left the nest to marry at a fairly young age) so at its peak, it really had only four occupants. Hillcrest, like most houses then, had no central heating. Each room had a coal fire-place but only the living room and the Raeburn in the kitchen had coal in them to heat the whole house. 'Frosted glass' was therefore a winter feature in not just the bathroom window, but all the bedrooms as the cold of winter was reflected in the ice forming on the windows from the inside!

TVs were pretty rare and colour TVs were rarer, but John Logie Baird's brilliance was reflected in the Rodgers' living room in colour in the late 1960s. 'Bill and Ben the Flowerpot Men', 'Tales from the Riverbank' and 'Andy Pandy' gave way to 'Blue Peter', 'Dixon of Dock Green', 'The White Heather Club' and 'Para Handy', and eventually, the advent of BBC2 and American TV shows like 'The High Chaparral'. TV was a great source of leisure and a bit of learning.

At work in the cemetery Dad took a great pride in seeing that the plots (grass) were cut neat and tidy and the rows of plots were as level as possible, by backfilling newer graves, which sunk when the earth recently returned to the graves compacted. Helping my Dad in the cemetery was a natural way of helping pay back my Mum and Dad's support. After all, if it was good enough for Rod Stewart[*], it was good enough for me. We could fill in a grave in about twenty-five minutes and have the wreaths neatly positioned, ready for the relatives and friends returning to see them. The heavy roller on the ATCO mower gave the grass those straight lines, which you rarely see nowadays, except on bowling greens and some football pitches. The old tell-tale lines were erased as the roller mower succumbed to 'less bother with a hover'.

Filling in graves and cutting grass was a breeze, but digging a grave by hand was hard, sweaty work. Even in death I think I would get claustrophobic in my wooden suit and therefore, it's the crematorium for me (when I go!?). A hole, six feet deep by around two feet wide at 'the shoulders' is not much room to work in and the deeper you go, the harder it is to throw the dirt out. New graves go to six feet and 're-open' to about four feet, six inches. I liked digging the graves, but my Dad would only let me dig down to about four feet before he would finish it off. Keen to finish off the digging for my Dad, on a day he had hurt his back quite badly, I kept digging to finish the job. It was a 're-open' and I came to the lid of the coffin of the previous burial. This was obviously deep enough, so I started to 'square off the shoulders' and sides, when I suddenly dropped a good foot into the grave which filled with musty air. I was mortified and was out of the hole like a sprinter out of running blocks – only vertically. The lid of the first coffin, after twenty years in the ground, had given way – after that, I wasn't too keen to dig beyond four feet.

Mum went up and down the street every day, except Sunday, and 'lugged' messages all week. Friday, being payday, was special and fruit and bars of 'Five-boys Chocolate' could be had. Instead of a fridge or a freezer, in those days we had a pantry. It was the equivalent of a large walk-in wardrobe for

---

[*] Apparently after a trip to Paris Rod started as a grave digger at the Highgate graveyard but he only stayed a couple of weeks; hardly a record but then he had other records to make.

storing food. Ground space would be used for potatoes (normally half-a-hundred weight, or fifty-six pounds, or twenty-five kilos in Euro measurement), carrots, turnips and other vegetables. The lower, cooler shelves would be reserved for meat and fish, and cereals and items used regularly would be at hand or eye level shelves for ease of use. Cooking was a major activity for my Mum and most of it in the early days was done on the Raeburn, a sort of coal-fired cooker, which also served to heat up the kitchen where, on the pulley, damp clothes would also be dried.

Food or fruit was the last thing on our minds when we received a huge parcel from my cousin William Kerr, who was serving with the RAF in Gann, an island in the Indian Ocean. However, the bugger had downed a coconut, complete with husks, and sent it to us in a box. William was Margaret's boy (Mum's sister) and he was a bit special, even if the coconut was a bit of an anti-climax – but I don't suppose there were many gift shops on Gann.

Kilmarnock Football Club versus Leeds United in the Fairs Cup in 1967 was the first senior football match I ever attended. Killie were at their peak and the ground seemed filled to capacity. The game passed me by as I jostled and jumped up and down – not in celebration of a goal, but in an effort to get a glance of the park and players. All seated stadiums definitely benefit the 'wee man'.

Adolescence is a funny thing and I think I knew I was in it when I paid more attention to the new French student teacher's legs than her lessons – and I liked French! It was then French ceased to be a language and became a kiss. It's about this time that boys experience 'learning difficulties' and girls experience difficult boys. Adolescence was all the more pronounced when we moved to Newmilns School and there were a whole new range of female faces and figures to contend with.

Discos at the Club (Darvel Juniors' Social Club, now demolished), Boy Scouts, Girl Guides and birthday parties all provided opportunities to slow dance to 'Je t'aime', 10cc's 'I'm Not In Love' etc, and have a good snog on the way home or to the bus stop. It was like underwater swimming, without the snorkel – you just held your breath and went for it.

Our immediate family reached its peak but we acquired an extended family as Lilian married wee Duncan McTavish. Marlene, after 'going out' with a few guys – including one who was deaf (I should add that he was deaf *before* he met Marlene) – married Big Frank Best from Galston (now there's a change from Wee Jock, Wee Eck, Wee Kenny!). Elaine married Alistair McKie and that became an extended family in itself, as there were eight (Jack, Alistair, George, Andy, Margaret, Mary, Susan and Morag) in Alistair's immediate family. Jim and Jessie tied the knot on 26th September 1975 – a significant date for reasons yet to unfold. Too young to attend the first two weddings of Lilian and Duncan and Marlene and Frank, I was in Gowanbank Hotel in Darvel to see Elaine and Alistair married and at Crofthead Farm Restaurant for Jim and Jessie's wedding. Bobby and myself ended up legless at Jim and Jessie's 'do' as we raced 'hauf for hauf' and later adjourned to Hillcrest with the family only to throw up and awake to a massive hangover.

Even in the 1970s, Scotland was enlightened when it came to a question of where and when people could be married. Next to the 'Best Man', the Minister was the 'main man' in terms of agreeing to particular locations for weddings. Gowanbank Hotel was originally the ancestral home of the Morton's who were instrumental in establishing the lace manufacturing in Darvel. Crofthead Farm and Restaurant is no more, as 'green belt' was buckled by houses to form part of the hamlet of Priestland.

The location of these marriages in a sense was absolutely meaningless – it was all about what was shared then between the bride and groom and how it would stand the test of time, fortune, family and forbearance that really mattered.

My Mum is absolutely Christian in her values but literally had little time for those that Robert Burns epitomised in 'Holy Willie's Prayer'. Living the life was more important than being there on a Sunday and singing the song in your finest apparel. My Mum of course would not actually say this, but I have no such sensitivities. That is not to say there were not, and are not, genuine Christian people about – even in Darvel. One of those was undoubtedly Mr Collins, who stayed at the Manse. He was the Minister who married most of our family. He was a *real* Christian, but a hellish driver, from whom even folk on crutches would refuse a lift!

As he drove along the road, he would attend to his flock – he would wave to Mrs Anderson, beckon to Johnnie James and move to greet the new Rodgers' baby on the other side of the road. God knows how he passed his test and God must have kept a powerful eye on him, because for all of his motoring meanderings, he was only involved in two minor accidents in his red Mini. Collins Court now stands near the centre of Darvel and is fittingly named in memory of Mr Collins, who is our, and Scotland's, longest-serving Parish Minister ever – and ever, Amen.

In 1971, I ventured to 'L.A.' as that was the year the brand-spanking new (or belting) Loudoun Academy opened its doors (on 26 February 1971) to the cream of the learning talent from Darvel, Newmilns, Galston and Hurlford. If Galston was the 'historical heart of Ayrshire and the home of the Campbells of Loudoun Castle', Hurlford struck fear into the heart of Ayrshire, and was the home of Big Joe Haining, Widzy, the Hamiltons and the McCanns. This is of course the stuff local legends are made of and Hurlford is the equal of any of the Irvine Valley towns. Perception is however reality and the perception was that Hurlford was viewed as a rough and tough town, but with good people in it, who had lovely daughters who were much sought after by 'gentlemen' from the 'higher-level' Valley towns – particularly Darvel!

Apart from Elaine's stint at College, no Rodgers had stayed on at school beyond the earliest leaving date. There were jobs out there and the money was needed in the house. My decision to stay on at school was never questioned by Mum and Dad, just supported. In the scheme of things anyway, if I had left school then I would have been destined to become a 'candlestick maker' – after all, Bobby was a butcher with William Allans and Sons, Jim a baker with the Co-op, so that only left the one occupation according to the old nursery rhyme. On the female side of the family, Lilian had started a family of her own, Marlene worked in the lace industry in Jock Aird's factory, and Elaine became a secretary within BMK in Kilmarnock (the once world renowned carpet makers).

Jobs were the last thing on my mind as we lined up against 'The Jo's' (St Joseph's Academy, Kilmarnock) in the final of the Ayrshire Cup at Rugby Park, home of Kilmarnock FC. Big Jim McFadzean, one of the 1965 League Winners' legends, had decked us out in an old black-and-white hooped Ayr United strip, which reached my knees. On a winter's day it would have made a great 'willie-warmer' but on a summer's evening it was a sweater! Still, some of us froze on the evening and 'The Jo's' deservedly won 3-0 with Paddy Brolly and Michael Joyce running the show. It was really hard to take the defeat but my days with Ernie 'Broon's' Youth Club football team should have prepared me for it. Penalty misses are even harder to take, especially when it is down to you and in the Youth Club Cup Final, I had missed a penalty to win the game, and Tony Wright missed the penalty to lose the game. The school Cup Final was worse than that, with family, friends and fellow pupils all turning out for the game. Still, we received a standing ovation at the assembly the next day.

Sport (unlike today it seems) featured very strongly in school life – everything from football, rugby, running, cross-country running, basketball, volleyball and even cricket. Everything but swimming, which was out of my league – forty-five feet of my fifty feet swimming badge was underwater and I think I walked twenty of those! Fortunately, the sports championship was decided on 'terra firma' and following on from John and Hugh Collins, Kenny Mann and myself became the Senior Boys Sports Champions in 1974. It was competitive 'stuff' – you ran a race to win it, not just to be in it. Other kids with less sporting prowess had talents to demonstrate, be it academically, in art, music, chess – these talents were honed and exhibited in a competitive environment, not in a world of over-protective 'everyone's a winner' mediocre mentality. Everyone's a winner if they compete and develop whatever talent they believe they have.

1973–4 was also a good year for football. As 16-year olds, Tony Wright and myself (that well-known penalty missing double act) joined Newmilns Vesuvius Amateurs. It was a star 'studded' line up, including Jackie and Benny Ferrie, Billy Fulton, John Guild, Billy McMillan, Rab Struthers, Jock Spence and James McAllister – among others. The mighty Knockentiber (the 'Tiber') were trounced 4-2 as Vesuvius lifted the Ayrshire Cup. Tony and I didn't feature (probably for fear of going to penalties), but 'we were there', and we were part of it – including the celebrations in the Crown Hotel in Newmilns.

'We were there' was also the cry for the Scotland vs. Czechoslovakia game in 1973, when Big Jim Holton and Joe Jordan did the business and got Scotland through to the World Cup Finals. The experience of the hair on the back of your neck and head standing on edge in national pride and fervour is one to be savoured, but someone pissing down the back of your jacket and legs is not (although the hot sensation at the start is not entirely unpleasant!).

Scarborough was the first place I went on holiday to, other than visiting relatives for one or two days. This was neither surprising nor disappointing – we would have needed a ten or twelve-berth caravan if we were all to go on holiday together. Steve Fullarton's (*aka* Big Steve) Mum and Dad took us to the delights of Scarborough. The bed and breakfast place was conveniently situated over the pub and there was a fish and chip shop just down the road. This could probably be said for every B & B in Scarborough, but at the time, it seemed unique. The 'shows', the gardens and Robin Hood's Bay (I'm assured he came out of Sherwood Forest and stripped to his Lincoln green trunks just outside Scarborough) were all the source of enjoyment. Yet the evenings were a source of mystery – would we get served in a pub? No chance! Would we pull the burdz? Very little chance! Would we try and fail? Every chance! Having tried and failed on both 'pubbing' and 'pulling', we resorted to the picture house. We got into an 'X-rated' picture without a dirty 'Mac' and watched the *'menage-a-trois'* unfold – Big Steve was baffled but luckily, I had stuck in at French. As the lights went up and we tried to creep out with the other creeps, we spied two smashing young 'lassies', who would obviously be hot for it. Our trail in pursuit of the smashers went cold after ten minutes and we raced up the road only to get into a row for being late.

Some meticulous planning the next year and the dream team (me, Alan Kerr, Stevie (Gillies), Big Steve Fullerton, Colin McLaren and Melly) went by 'Golden Rail' to Bournemouth. 'Golden Rail', now there's nostalgia for you and the modern day equivalent is probably 'Rusty or Broken Rail'. Bournemouth in the '70s was a haven for foreign students and the Bee Hive disco was a real 'honey pot'. Swedish, Norwegian and French language students were all the rage and we all had a measure of success in the language of love – some measures were bigger than others but – what the Hell.

The other side to holidays was that my Mum and Dad could never really take a holiday – there were all those kids to be looked after. But this changed in the early 1970s, when Marlene was old enough to look after the family when my Mum and Dad succumbed to the lure of Lloret de Mar, at £39 per person per week as their one and only holiday abroad (excluding Southern Ireland). My Mum and Dad survived the broken down coach and last gasp effort to board the plane; too much sun and food for which they had no real appetite. It was an adventure and experience with friends, but one they have never repeated, through a combination of choice and necessity. We survived a week 'home alone' with the minor crime count of:

One burnt hearth carpet;

One burn to Yvonne's back;

One broken window;

Two bloody noses (Bobby one – Kenny one),

And a realisation of how much we missed our Mum and Dad.

As the time drew nearer for the seniors to leave school and we became more 'mature', we (Kerr, McLaren, Stevie Gillies, me and a few other dubious but artistic characters) decided to give the Prefects' Room a 'makeover' – we were obviously well before our times and 'Changing Rooms'.

Nowadays, the seniors leaving school have a prom and attend in stretch limos, all dolled up to the nines. No such luck (or money) then so the 'makeover' would be our parting gift to the school and the new prefects. Andy Warhol would have been proud, as things had got out of hand. Images, expressions, cartoons and jokes adorned every wall before spray painting became regarded as 'art'. Where beige paint once reigned supreme, a rainbow of colours and rash of jokes appeared. The word got out the guys were painting the Prefects' Room red... green... blue... yellow... pink... purple and any other colour they could get their hands on or make.

Sitting happy and in a state of near post-coital contentment (which you could tell from the whiff of smoke in the room), we surveyed our finished work. Genius! Sheer, bloody genius! Then the SAS, in the shape of Mr Paton (the Deputy Head) and two of his Stormtroopers, bounded in unannounced, uninvited and unwelcome, but also unimpressed. They were at the same time amazed and aghast at the sight which befell them. Paton shook his head in anguish and despair and looked to the heavens (ceiling) for salvation, only to see a huge nude figure winking back at him in all her glory.

Our Prefects badges were duly surrendered and the room was locked until the painters could restore the décor, or even the decorum. It was rumoured that the teachers were given guided tours of the room and at least some of them were impressed by the artwork and others learned a whole new range of words and phrases. The room was restored to its brilliant beige best and refilled with 'beige people' as Billy Connolly would have it.

With seven 'O' levels (six A's and one B) and five Highers (four Bs and one C), sealed and delivered by Royal Mail, my ambition was to be a 'drillie'. Jordanhill College offered a Diploma in Physical Education to a very limited number of applicants each year and, at seventeen, I sought out one of the places. Having been told to return the following year and get an eyesight test, I discovered that time and the glasses helped my myopia, both in terms of sight and future opportunities. Jordanhill would not be the subject of a future attempted entry, as Edinburgh, Glasgow and Strathclyde Universities were all assessed as future places of academic study. The grey matter was exercised as to which of these proud institutions would be my 'alma mater', and, in the end, after a further year at Loudoun completing Sixth year Studies (English and History), I plumped for Glasgow. It had a good pedigree and more of my mates were going there anyway.

These years of learning was summarised in three bits of paper – passports to learning, which spoke a bit for you but portrayed none of the struggle behind their acquisition. Mum and Dad were the foundations of my learning; their support fuelled my ambition 'to go on'. Significant contributors to my learning and development at Loudoun were Big Jim McFadzean, Dunky McBean, Wee Eck and Bill Clark, who in his John Noakes-style grey/green Mini Clubman, in true Blue Peter style, used to shepherd us all over the country in our games for Kilmarnock Hockey Club. Other characters included Rab Ellis and Mr Paton, who were 'real belters' with a wicked sense of timing, i.e. for catching you 'at it'. Back then, as now, the perennial problem for teachers was how to gain the respect of pupils without losing authority and academic achievement. Teachers then, as now, and not surprisingly, seemed to be an educational extension of their own personalities. The dull and grey people taught in dull and grey and those with a zest for life reflected this in their lessons.

Hockey, with the support of Bill Clark and the PE team, really took off at Loudoun from being a 'girls' game to a fast and skilful male pursuit. Casper, Big Fully, Stevie Gillies, Kenny Hunter, Kerr, Kenny Mann, Melly and myself were all part of the once thriving Kilmarnock Hockey Club, which played in the national leagues up until the late seventies. Hockey was also a sociable sport, so we began drinking 'a little' to be sociable and the more we played, the more sociable we became. Selection for South West Scotland U18 followed but the full Scotland jersey and cap eluded the two or three of us in the Regional team. Sociality can have its price!

Leaving Loudoun was funny, sad and totally unheralded; no fanfare, no celebration – just out there and no going back. The comfort of the local red brick was about to be exchanged for the queries in the quadrangle at Glasgow University. As far as Loudoun Academy was concerned, I was history and a new chapter was about to begin at the Uni.

The Western SMT bus drew into Glasgow's Anderston Street Bus Station in September 1975 (I think it had left Darvel sometime in August!). Stevie Gillies and myself, luggage in hand, jump off to climb up the north face of Blythswood Street and seek out Dalrymple Hall of Residence on Belhaven Terrace, just off Great Western Road. The Botanical Gardens, Westerlands Sports grounds, the BBC at Queen Margaret Drive, Byres Road, the Grosvenor Hotel, Studio 1, Queen Margaret Union and Glasgow University Union, were all within staggering distance of 'the Hall'.

Initially, the lure of home and long-standing friends was pretty strong, but new friendships were soon established and activities and relationships were formed, which meant returning home each weekend became less and less a feature. Friends at home became fewer and 'more distant'. Memories that tethered old friendships together were set loose in the face of new friendships, which thrived on being flung together from the four corners of Ayrshire and beyond.

With 'brass in pocket' – in the form of the maximum grant available – Uni life would be sweet. The maximum grant with maximum deductions for Hall fees, books, meals outwith the hall, clothes etc, meant minimum spending money and ongoing reliance and support from Mum and Dad.

'Freshers' Week' at Uni is the week before the formal commencement of one's studies, during which all the new first year intakes get pissed and get the piss taken out of them. Stevie and myself missed 'Freshers' Week' but caught up with our fellow Freshers at the Hall (at that time and all-male establishment). The 'Hall' contained a large contingent of Ayrshire men and 'Tuechters' (mainly from Dornoch, Brora, Golspie and Helmsdale) in about equal measure and this largely set the tone of the activities in the Hall. The main characters soon emerged – Big Al (the goalie – better than Andy Goram but a 'ginger' or 'fair-headed ginger'). Horm and Wee Jimmy (Horm's brother) from Stewarton, Jimmy Auld, Jim the boxer from Irvine (no change there then), John McHale, John Fife, Jim McCaffrey, Sid, Horrible Joe, Paul, Steve, Charlie Mitchell, John and Willie Young (the well-known masons in the black, otherwise referred to as football referees), and The Doc (Doctor Alan Scotney) was the Hall Warden who had a penchant for fine wines and malts, which he shared in gay abandon with the 'Hall Committee' and anyone else who might be in dire need of a wee refreshment!).

Glasgow had moved on from its 'no mean city' days and was entering 'cultural puberty', but for all that, you could still get a 'good doin' for nothing – the cry in Glasgow's case was,

'Whit wis that fur?'

Answer: '*Don't be fuckin cheeky or I'll gie ye whit fur!*'

Five years residence in Glasgow produced one good' tanning' (not of the Tommy Sheridan variety) and two near misses.

Scene 1, Take 1 –

Wearing a full-length denim coat and looking like a dick-head, whilst walking through Glasgow via the University Union early in the morning is a recipe for being set upon – and so it happened early doors in Glasgow. Me and Melly set against five hoodlums in search of a 'donation' to help them through the night. We didn't quite manage to talk them into giving us money but persuaded them we were as skint as they were and narrowly avoided a kicking on a sympathy vote.

Ingredients for a party success include plenty of booze, women, spacious accommodation, some food and decent music.

Scene 2, Take 1 –

At John Dempster's flat, we had the lot – it would be a good night. Things to avoid even at a good party in Glasgow – letting gatecrashers in, wearing a green shirt, and having the temerity to ask a 'big yin' to 'cool it', a la Henry Kissinger. The party gear was jeans and my bright green Kilmarnock Hockey Club top; the party gatecrasher was a 'big bruiser' but seemed a nice guy in the very dimly lit lounge. The kitchen was the stock area for the booze and was brightly lit, and true to form, there's always a 'party in the kitchen'.

'*Hey you.*'

'*Who me?*'

'*Yeah you, fuck face – were you wearing that green fuckin' rag when I was talking to you?*'

'*Aye, how? Do you think I've got a wardrobe to make a quick change at parties?*'

Gulp, my mistake trying wit and charm.

'Ya cheeky wee bastard, whit are ye wearin' that fur?'

'It's just a shirt – what's the problem?'

Gulp, mistake number two, as 'love Mum/Dad' and 'love Rangers' tattoos become evident. Beat hasty retreat to dimly lit lounge area and melt back in with the crowd. All quiet?! Back through to the kitchen for a beer, oh no, the 'big bigot's having a go at Melly and the party host, who politely asked, *'Who invited you anyway?'*

The 'big bigot' struggles with a name and starts to turn nasty.

'I'll do the pair of you.'

Enter yours truly.

'Cool it, big man, nae hassle?'

As a bottle meant for me cracks open Johns' head, I duck and he steps forward. The big man holds the top of the broken bottle and seems to attempt the New Zealand 'haka' to ward off anyone crazy enough to approach him or try and prevent him leaving – he drops his weapon and flees. The police and ambulance attend, just another Saturday night scene in Glasgow and the 'big bigot' retreats to his lair.

Ingredients of almost certain party failure are too few (good-looking) women, too many guys, some more guys without a carry-out, and some mean guys with a carry-out, who don't feel much like sharing it voluntarily.

Scene 3, Take 1

Another victory at the 5-asides and a few beers downed and big Broon knows where there's a party he can get us into along Great Western Road – no problem. Broon, John Fyfe, Big Al, Jim McCaffrey, Horrible Joe and yours truly – minus carry-out – gain entry to the 'party'. It was dire, even before 'Dire Straights' became famous – essential ingredients were all missing and it had all the ingredients for some 'stag rutting' - there was going to be trouble. We 'sneaked' a can each and when rumbled, claimed it as our own – the scene was set – out of the blue corner emerged a tough guy from Ayrshire and it wasn't me. Faced with 'flight or fight', I chose fight, but only after the tough guy and two of his mates had set about me. A punch and two boots to my head were shrugged off as Fyfe came to the rescue and dived on the back of one of the assailants. The hearth of the open coal fire seemed like a good place to get rid of the other two assailants and, whilst 'shite doesn't burn', it fairly melts with the heat.

Calm was restored and we strolled back to Dalrymple. My face felt like a £100 bill that had been accrued in the dentist's chair without the aid of an anaesthetic, as my lips, jaws, and gradually my eyes, all swelled up and numbed.

'You're not looking too smart, Kenny; is it sore?' says the concerned Jim.

'I'm o.... and f.....f....but.........,' I replied.

Early morning light brought the realisation that I would not have looked out of place at the Panda's party in the zoo. The foot mark on my forehead indicated the assailant was a size ten, and was unlikely to be a fan of Hush Puppies. I missed three days of lectures and tutorials as I couldn't face the outside world with a face which had all hallmarks and heelmarks of amateur cosmetic surgery. Paul the vet (he may have been a doctor) gave me some cream to take away the swelling and remove the multi-coloured bruising from my head and face.

As luck would have it, my 'kickin'' coincided with the end of my relationship with a 'big blonde' (at least 5'6") from the Scottish History class, who was less than impressed by my juvenile joustings. In my three-day recuperation at the Hall, the bitch had taken up with a tall, aristocratic, artistic arsehole and dumped me. Scottish History is littered with such personal feuds and treachery!

The natural progression was from street fighting to the 'noble art' and Queensbury Rules. Boxing training was the hardest and most gruelling physical training I have been involved in. After six months of pugilist purgatory, my big nose, big ears and big teeth finally hit home to me – I already had all the attributes of a beaten boxer, so why not cut out the middle man and stop boxing?

Westerlands Sports Ground was the place to be for the sporty types at Uni. Now it's the place to be for those who can afford the houses, subsequently built there. Probably nearing the peak of my physical fitness, I joined a group of sprinters for training, under an up and coming coach called Frank Dick. Two hundred metre sets were recorded at under twenty-five seconds, with increasing rest periods, as the repetition increased. No-one in this group could reach the speed, elegance and stamina of the tall, dark-haired figure who finished the session as strong as he had started, whilst all others trailed in his wake – sharp by name and sharp by nature, Cameron Sharp was a flying machine and in a league of his own. Yet he had no peacock strut or disdainful glance for his toiling competitors. He knew he was miles better than us even in a two hundred metre race, but he didn't rub it in. His sights and training were set on winning European and Commonwealth medals, rather than University championships.

That one memorable training session taught me I'd never be a sprinter and so instead, I became a javelin thrower! If I had little to support even an amateur career in the boxing ring, or running, then I had even less to support my aspirations in the javelin – I was almost 5'7½" short and then weighed 10½ stone. The training sessions at Westerlands ended and getting a javelin home to Darvel to continue my training was no mean feat. The first leg of the journey was completed when Mark Brodie's Dad dropped me off at Brodie's Wee Thack in Kilmarnock (now the Brass and Granite). Looking like an extra from *Zulu*, I sauntered through Kilmarnock to the bus station, where the great debate ensued as to the javelin's eligibility to travel; the appropriate fare for the javelin, if it was eligible to travel?

'Right son, let's go.'

The silver spear was slotted along the length of the parcel shelf on the single decker at no cost – common sense prevailed. Third place at the Uni championships ended my javelin-throwing career.

Hampden Park, Glasgow, was the scene for the Scottish Junior Cup Final on 24 April 1976. Proud as punch I paid my 50p admission to the terraces and joined the Darvel contingent of the 20,161 spectators. I was there – I was there to watch 'Bo'ness beat brave little Darvel' 3–0. Darvel Juniors Social Club was a heaving mass of blue and white as the commiserations extended into the early hours of the morning as the reality of defeat dawned.

Hamilton College Football Park was the scene for the final of the 1977 McEnhill Cup Final between Hamilton College and Dalrymple Hall. There was no entry fee and we were watched by about eighty students and the obligatory 'dug'.

A determined Dalrymple Hall lifted the cup and in the 'Rock' off Byers Road, it was filled with whisky, vodka, lager Guinness and laughter. We won the cup! In 1978, we endeavoured to repeat the feat and came up against the oddly-named NECROS, who turned out to be more deadly in front of goal than Dalrymple. We lost the cup!

In 1977/8, the Glasgow Colleges Football Association (whose President was the aptly-named Tommy Docherty) proclaimed:

'The McEnhill Cup Final involved the intriguing clash between NECROS, the new league champions in their first season in the First Division, and Dalrymple, the McEnhill Cup holders. NECROS First Division experience counted in the end and the Second Division team had to settle for second place in the competition which they have come to think of (with some justification) as their own.'

Football trials at Jordanhill College, Glasgow, for the Glasgow College Select to play a Dutch team turned from the ecstasy of selection to the agony of realising torn knee ligaments meant the Dutch dream was over before it really began.

Social life at Uni was a mixture of feast and famine, interspersed with exams. At the start of the term, money seemed to be no object and exams seemed a long way off. It was time to live a little and the circle of 'bon viveurs' was large. As grants turned to debt and exams clouded the horizon, only the intelligent rich or the doomed to failure could maintain the social pace.

In the late 1970s, the pace of life seemed to quicken and change became the order of the day. Still, some things don't seem to change, as twenty-five years after the 'Green Goddesses' took to the streets in 1977, history has repeated itself with a second period of strike action by the Fire Brigades Union members. Back in January 1978, the Studio One Bar, off Byres Road, at the tip adjoining Great Western Road and the Grosvenor Hotel, was a favourite watering hole of the lads. In the early part of the first strike, it became a hole with water in it, as the valiant army fire-fighters failed to douse the initial flames and the fire took hold in the Grosvenor Hotel before being finally put out.

The world was further 'shaken up' after Elvis died on 16 August 1977.

However, 1978 also became a 'quiz question' year, as there were three popes 'inaugurated' – John Paul I dying after only thirty-three days in office.

As ever, it was a case of 'out with the old and in with the new' as the first test-tube baby was born in Oldham General Hospital in 1978.

The University Union (male dominated) and the Queen Margaret Union (female orientated) were the haunts of many a famous or infamous act. John Martyn went close to electrocuting himself on stage at the QMU and that was the highlight of the night. Hedgehog Pie was well remembered – if only for their name but Be Bop Deluxe at the GUU were magic, in a haze of sweet-smelling smoke; but funnily enough, their album was less impressive when listened to in a smoke-free environment! The GUU was also the early husting ground for young Charles Kennedy, current leader of the Liberal Democrats.

Punk music also spat onto the stage as safety pins and black bin bags became 'oh so pretty'. If music has to go 'underground', and reinvent itself every now and then, punk should have stayed there, or more accurately, most punks should have stayed there!

Taking a trip down memory lane can be refreshing, but with Glasgow's Asian influence, especially in the West End, we were encouraged to take a trip down 'Curry Alley' – Gibson Street. The Kohinoor, the Taj Mahal all seduced students with the prospect of a hot, spicy, cheap meal and a late drink. Be it a bhoona, madras or vindaloo, no self-respecting student staying in the West End of Glasgow could avoid the curry houses.

The *'modus operendi'* was to go out for a few pints (six to eight was advisable if you were a 'vindaloo virgin'); fail to 'get off' with anyone and drown your sorrows a bit more, then descend upon the curry house of your choice or, more accurately, the one you could afford.

The 'Koh' was the scene for Kerr's 21st birthday celebrations (now a celebrated lawyer in Kilmarnock!) It was a low-key affair – me and him! A few pints and an invitation to have a curry on him, I presumed. In the back of the 'Koh' the lamb bhoona was scoffed and a few pints more downed, when Kerr declares, *'How much have you got? I don't think I can cover this – we'll do a runner.'*

'Hold on, let's check; get the bill and then make a move,' I whispered, in a tone Quasimodo could have heard above the bells.

The bill is duly obtained and two pound notes quickly turn into four, through a strategic ripping and placing of change, we 'covered' the bill. No sooner had the money been 'double counted' and the birthday boy was out of the back room and gaining freedom at the main door. I followed and we laughed as the great escape had been brilliantly executed, without the aid of a motorbike. Ten yards from the Koh, the laughing stopped, as two waiters and a cook challenged our arithmetic and invited us to return to the Koh. A brief exchange of karate moves devoid of any contact and we legged it – we'd saved two pounds and been on the run two minutes after leaving the Koh, surely a record! Curries at the Koh were off the menu for a time after that.

Studying, or lack of studying, like restaurant waiters, eventually catches up with you. The book mileage and library silence pain barrier has to be gone through for the vast bulk of students. My Modern History and Scottish History Joint Honours Degree was exchanged for Political Economy (Economics) and Modern History, as the reality of two years of study began to bite – do you want to be history teacher? Answer – no. Then why the hell are you continuing with two history options? Answer – Political Economy (Economics). There were no problems with an ordinary degree and I could secure that in the normal three years, but the switch to Economics, part way through, meant a five-year (honours) course. Five years on top of 'O' levels and Highers meant my Mum and Dad had an extra burden for seven years beyond the norm of leaving school at sixteen, and with no return in sight. It was never questioned, never queried and always supported.

Members of the aristocracy in the 19th century were renowned for embarking on the 'Grand Tour' to seek enlightenment at first hand. Not to be outdone, Melly (Gordon Melrose) and myself embarked on our own 'Tour de France' – we would hitchhike round France in search of *je ne sais quoi.'*

A lift to and overnight stay at Melly's sister and brother-in-law's house in Hinckley (the centre of England) got us off to a free and flying start. Sixty fags secured a lift to Portsmouth and we were St Malo bound on the evening ferry. We were 'cool' as everyone scurried on board, no hassle, there was space for everyone. The reality was that good space was at a premium and on a first come, first served basis. We endured the crossing on deck, sprawled between wooden chairs with the sky and newspapers for blankets – boy we were 'cool'.

We got our bearings and stretched our legs out through the quaintly quaint St Malo until we were on the open French *autoroutes,* thumbing a lift anywhere, from anyone. The North of France was beautiful, with no appearance of affluence or industry. It was a relief from the West of Scotland, both in terms of the rural setting and the weather. Lifts in the North of France came fairly readily, even to two foreign blokes with big rucksacks. The French people there were open, communicative and generous. From St Malo, the happy wanderers went via Rheims and Nantes to St Jean de Monts. In our 'desire' to get somewhere, we went through Rheims and Nantes like an invading (or retreating) army and paid scant attention to their architecture or attractions. We reached our first destination at sundown and gazed along a long, sandy beach. This was a pleasure beach without the Blackpool distractions. This would do for us - if we could find somewhere to pitch the tent. Neither of us were boy scouts, so pitching the tent in a small wooded area, about a mile from the beach, in darkness, was a major achievement.

Early the next day, my French studies at Uni paid off, as we bought wine, cheese, bread and fruit and made our way to the beach, which had the night before seemed full of 'evening promise'. St Jean de Monts was a million miles from Darvel, and even further from Galston – by midday, the beach and cafes were the places to be seen and to see. We set up our al fresco picnic halfway along the beach, near to the freshwater shower area. The shower drew some unexpected benefits, as the *'jeune filles'* retired from the beach for lunch. It was the first beach I had been on, where the girls went topless and the water from the shower was obviously very cold – our picnic by the shower lasted much longer than our food and drink! As night fell, we enjoyed a beer and some smattered French conversation with the 'locals', from all over France, until the topic came round to where we were staying. Shit, the tent and our rucksacks were still in the woods, hopefully! A swift return and check and all was well, life was good in St Jean de Monts.

St Jean de Monts was pure relaxation, but after three days, the wanderlust was on us and we hit the road again. We hitched it to a campsite at La Rochelle, with its 'twin turrets' at the harbour entrance. After two days of taking in the sights and forking out on campsite fees, we moved on, to Bordeaux. Bordeaux was a world of difference from St Jean de Monts and La Rochelle and the Youth Hostel was a riot of nationalities, all trying to speak and impress each other, all at once. The linen and our bunks were secured and we enjoyed a chicken and chips 'menu fixe', with a bottle of Bordeaux. A brightly-lit shop drew our attention and we floated into it like moths to a light bulb. It was a 'sweetie shop', or at least, an adult sweetie shop and we fluttered round it, bumping into customers as our attention was drawn to an array of gismos and gadgets. It was the first sex shop I'd ever been in. Some of the rubber, leather and silk gear was so far out I could only imagine that the nuns in France were wearing the equivalent of Anne Summers party gear. Scotland, or so it seemed to us, was a mere backwater when it came to sex shops. We stayed long enough to satisfy our curiosity, but not long enough to let anyone think we were 'queer' – anyway, none of us wore earrings. 'Queer as folk' certainly took on a new meaning after our saunter through the sex shop.

Lifts were getting harder and harder to secure as we moved south and although the cars on the road seemed to be bigger and more expensive, the drivers were decidedly discerning when it came to picking up two male hitch hikers with their rucksacks. The old trick of one hitching at the road and the other out of immediate sight worked a treat (after eight hours!) and we arrived at Cassis after skirting through the menacing Marseilles and an overnight stay in Sete. Sete seemed like a combination of medieval England and Venice where local Sailors mounted gondolas on the canal and galloped towards each other by thrashing oars in the water and 'jousting' to send the blue or red champion into the murky water. With no obvious place to pitch a tent in Cassis, we followed the wooden cross AJ signs in search of the Youth Hostel. The wide dirt road became a narrow, rocky track and then a goat path and, after forty minutes, we saw the Youth Hostel in the distance, and looked back to what must be some of the best views in France – rockscapes, caves and trees, dropping back to the blue Mediterranean sea – artists could have a field day, so to speak. This was the Cassis the French poet Frederick Misteral exaggeratedly exclaimed 'he who has seen Paris and not Cassis has seen nothing at all'. In travel brochures and tourist speak it would read, 'Cassis, a little seaside resort nestled at the foot of the impressive Cape Canaille Cliff. A former Roman trading post, Cassis is very charming with its quays lined with cafés, jagged little coves and beaches.' What it wouldn't say is that the youth hostel is three miles out of town and up every inch of Cape Canaille which are Europe's highest sea cliffs.

We were parched and in my best attempt at French, I asked where we could get a drink of water. *'Over there, second door on the right, straight through and first door on the left.'* Melly sat on a small wall, catching his breath, as I followed the directions given. I sipped water from a drinking fountain as I realised I was in a shower unit – a shower unit from which the most beautiful girl emerged 'starkers'. *Ca va,* I gasped and continued to drink and drink and drink. *Ca va bien,* indeed. 'Starkers' is a particularly Scottish word, but it doesn't do credit to this French masterpiece. In my mind's eye and memory, she was a 36-24-36 brunette, shaking rivulets of water from her frame, before the towel was grasped and patted to her body. I recall she was 'an evenly roasted chicken' with none of the usual 'white bits' to break her overall tan and this just added to the sleek continuity of her natural body curves.

I emerged in the sunlight to a burst of laughter, which even Melly joined in – it had been a set-up. In our three days at Cassis, I only ever saw my vision of loveliness once – it turned out she was the hostel manager's wife and he was a big guy, so it was a case of dream on and move on.

Strasbourg, now the home of the European Parliament, was our next real stop. It had real character and was really expensive, even then. We curtailed our cultural tours and made off in search of a lift.

We were dropped off on the outskirts of Saarbruken, which is on the French-German border and as darkness fell, we found a right quiet, grassy spot, with some shrubbery all round. It felt as if we had hardly slept at all, when the nice quiet spot became noisier and noisier. Curiosity got the better of me. I ambled off in a state of undress, through the shrubbery to discover we had pitched the tent on a huge roundabout! Still, it was the ideal place to recommence our hitch hiking!

We had started our 'grand tour' with around £80 and needed about £20 to get a Transalpino train ticket from Paris, ferry crossing to Dover, and train to London, where Melly's brother would put us up for a night. After fifteen days, Youth Hostels and campsites were out of our league. With not even a 'roundabout' to pitch the tent on, we made ourselves comfortable in a bus shelter on the outskirts of Saarbruken. After the initial roar of motor bikes and cars died down, we got off to sleep. The bus shelter was of the old metal style, all the way to the ground, with no gaps for cold air and only one entrance to the right of where I was sleeping. A light padding noise, interrupted by sloshing sounds on the front of the shelter, awoke me. The padding and the sloshing worked round behind me and up and down the shelter – this was weird. My first thoughts were a dog, but it soon became evident that there was at least one person involved in the activity – whatever it was, I kicked Melly awake and in my best sign language, alerted him to the potential intruder(s). By now, I was standing up with a glass bottle ready to defend myself, from whatever was out there, as it was now evident it was working its way round the shelter and was now intent on exploring the bus shelter with evil in mind!?

A tall figure moved to enter the shelter with one weapon in each hand and I rose to the challenge; *'Whit the fuck do you think you're doing?'* – My command of French had temporarily left me. The guy, with a bucket and brush, blurted in French we should leave the bus shelter. A quick *'Get tae fuck or I'll stick your brush up your "derrière"'* persuaded him to leave us to our beauty sleep. A quick look with the torch revealed he had been 'decorating' the bus shelter with illegal, political posters. After that, I was convinced that 'Bill stickers should be prosecuted'.

A French civil engineer, visiting his relatives in Saarbruken, took us all the way to Paris and even dropped us off at the *Gard du Nord,* from where we could get a train to Calais and then the ferry to Dover. We arrived too late to purchase our Transalpino ticket and to secure our only remaining money for the tickets, we 'rented' a big locker to hold both rucksacks. With only a few francs in hand, we would have a crepe (pancake) and a coffee and stroll through *'gay Paree'*, before sleeping in the *Gard du Nord*. About midnight, the station security guards pleasantly opened the doors for us to explore the city. In the café bar, I worked out we couldn't have a crepe, only coffee. This was duly ordered and we sat down, only to be faced with a bill we could not pay – with a great hullabaloo, the coffee was removed and we were told in no uncertain terms to get out. So much for French hospitality, we thought, before a bold French knight came to our rescue, bought us a beer, and explained he would put us up for the night – no problem. Halfway up the stairs to his flat, the concierge – the equivalent of the worst Blackpool landlady you can think of – said, and I quote, *'Where the fuck do you think you are going with those two twats?'* A quick sorry from the not-so-bold knight, and it was good night to the 'two twats'.

Making our way back to the *Gard du Nord* was an uneasy trip at 1.30 a.m. Men in black – not Will Smith – seemed to emerge, first one to the right, then two to the left, and one behind. We were stick-out tourists and these guys looked like serious French-Algerian henchmen in full length black leather coats. The threat seemed real, and I alerted Melly, and our walk across the square quickened, so it appeared did that of the four potential assailants. The threat increased as the square began to taper off and the exit point was the likely attack point. We were worried, big time. From behind rang out *La Marseillaise* and eight French Paratroopers in full gear jumped up in our direction. *'Get fell in, Melly – stick with these guys, wherever they're going.'* So we joined the 'Foreign Legion' for about two hours and the men in black leather coats merged into the darkness like some black shadows of the Gestapo in days gone by.

The rendezvous point for the Paratroopers was the *Gard du Nord* – a wee touch of luck at last. The station security personnel, who so politely and obligingly let us out of the station, would not allow re-entry at around 2.30 a.m. – not even armed with eight French Paratroopers. The Paras hunkered down for the remainder of the night at the entrance to the railway station and Melly and me followed suit. Snuggled together with our new-found Para friends, we had survived all that Paris could throw at us. In adversity, this was our *Arc du Triumph*.

An incessant tapping of metal to stone and a tap on the shoulder from the Para next to me and I realised Paris had more to throw at us. Dressed in red, real synthetic leather, stood the oldest pro from the oldest profession in the world. She gesticulated and beckoned and as each eye opened, blinked in disbelief, and closed, she moved along the 'Maginot' line. If Chris de Burgh had seen this old dear, then 'Lady in Red' would never have seen the light of day! There were no takers, but the Paras were now moved to action. A quick reconnoitre had spied an open window, which was reachable via drainpipes, up two outbuildings. One Para, two Paras, made it up and in, and just as I was thinking, I don't fancy this much, the first Para opened an emergency exit and the troops flooded in. In the warmth of the station, we relaxed and reflected on what might have been.

Transalpino came up trumps the next day, and the journey to London went off without a hitch. A phone call from Melly to his brother and we were on the right bus to go and stay with him overnight. The suggestion to get a fish supper was politely declined – the offer to pay for it was readily accepted. A cholesterol special after seventeen days on bread, cheese, fruit and wine wouldn't kill us. We hitch hiked separately and uneventfully to Scotland. We had done it and to complete our education, it was back to Uni.

If France had been a bit of a culture shock, then returning to Uni was shocking. Studying and people became more intense. For some, the Peter Pan or genial gypsy world continued; for others, finals and fiancés beckoned. The sight of the super six (me, Big Al, JY (John Young), Willie Young, Charlie Mitchell and Gus) in Shotts on a Friday afternoon at 4.00 p.m. was too much for most of the locals. Dressed in our best 'Saturday Night Fever' suits, with flares to sweep the streets, we swept into town in search of the Co-op Hall. Tommy Buggy, a 'ginger' and chemistry graduate, was marrying a Brazilian. Shotts Bon Accord 1, Brazil 0, an unlikely result, we thought, as we strolled through Shotts with our pre evening invitation fish suppers. *'Aye son, up the street, sandstone building on the left, up the stairs, ye canny miss it,'* and we were welcomed to a wedding which was a cross between a ceilidh and a samba – a real *'Ceilamba.'*

The Latinos were easily recognisable from the pale-faced Buggy entourage. In the calm of the early evening, the Brazilian family sang a beautiful 'lullaby of Rio' and in return, not to be outdone by 'those foreigners', we gave a late-night rendition of 'Flower of Scotland'. Shotts Bon Accord - aye right!

In my best (only) grey suit, with wide jacket lapels and extravagant flared trousers, and full of the drink, I fancied my chances. Tommy's bride had a sister and she was gorgeous.

'*Aye son, go for it*' was the cry as I tried my best dancing steps (two forward, two back) and command of the French language on the heavenly sister of the bride. No luck with the dancing, no luck with the French; '*Do you speak English,*' she enquired? '*Not very well, but I'll give it a go – I'm Kenny Rodgers, but I don't sing and you are beautiful.*' The patter went downhill from there, but there was a bit of a spark and an offer of staying at Tommy's sisters, before the demon drink kicked in. '*No, I had to see the lads home.*' – What a prick! A Brazilian belle on my lap, and I blew it! In your dreams, son, in your dreams!

We crammed into Gus's car and he drove back to Glasgow, as *Super tramp* blared out of the car stereo. We stopped on the way for last orders but drink and dreams had got the better of me. I was left sleeping in the car. It was a seminal moment and sign of the times; all around, people were graduating in their education and life, as engagement was followed by marriage.

On the immediate family front, things seemed normal with no big upheavals from my perspective. It was a time when I was really, in a sense, not a full part of the family. Events happened but I had no real conception on the thinking and feelings of my brothers and sisters to these events, as my contact with them had become less over my period of study at University.

I also had no real conception of how close I could have been to losing my eldest brother, Jim, who had contracted meningitis. A lumbar puncture and hospital treatment had saved his life.

By the end of the '70s, Lilian had moved to Sandford and she and Duncan had four kids. Jim and Jessie had two kids; Marlene and Frank stayed in Galston and Lorraine was their first and only offspring. Elaine and Alistair had 'Kevin the infant'. Yvonne had a job in Curtaincraft; David worked for Mappin and Webb, the jewellers in Kilmarnock, and Colin made pallets in a woodworker's yard in Newmilns. Avril and Graham were the last two at school/Loudoun Academy. Like our forefathers, there was nothing exotic, nothing absolutely unique in terms of our individual lives and careers.

A new era was about to dawn and a new (or old) political creed had been spawned. The Tories came to power – the film that followed was a 'PG' – 'personal greed'. As far as Scotland was concerned, the Tory leader, Margaret Thatcher was MT (empty) and the PT (poll tax) was unacceptable. Nevertheless, we and the nation endured eighteen years of 'Tory rule'. 'Francis of Assisi' managed to simultaneously join and split the nation(s) in one fell swoop of the archangel Thatcher.

Irrespective of political loyalties, the late 1970s changed my world and my family for ever. Being a best man at a wedding can be a nerve-racking experience and all the more so if you are on a 'semi-blind' date at the same time. Within a week or so of Stevie (Gillies) and Yvonne's (Milroy) wedding, I found myself without a partner. My sister Yvonne came to the rescue – Nancy McCulloch, who worked with Yvonne, would accompany me as best man at the wedding. We had precious little time before or even during the wedding to speak, as we were seated at separate tables in the Hunting Lodge in Kilmarnock. The 'semi-blind' date stemmed from the fact we had both been at Loudoun Academy, but Nancy was two years younger than me. The wedding went well but ended not with a dance, but with everyone retreating to their own individual house parties. Without a car, we left Stevie's Mum and Dad's party in full swing and set off for our buses home. It had been an eventful, uneventful day. There was no immediate spark or suggestion of romance, but enough of an attraction and interest to have a 'full-sighted' date.

Mavis (Patricia) and Harry were Nancy's Mum and Dad and, as the 'Cinderella', she had three 'ugly sisters' – Trisha, Jeanette and Marion. In truth, the three would be a catch for any aspiring suitor, and the only Cinderella in Hurlford was the Cinderella Pub (now the Poacher's Rest).

In marriage terms, four daughters were a nightmare for Nancy's Mum and Dad, as they would have to pay for all their weddings to follow. On Armistice Day in 1977, a truce was struck and Trisha, Nancy's eldest sister, exchanged her vows with John Collins, as a long Loudoun Academy association came to fruition after years of 'winching'. Nancy was the lone bridesmaid.

The descendants of the Rodgers and McCullochs were pretty similar.

The McCulloch's generally came from smaller families (not entirely surprising, when compared to the Rodgers, although Harry was the youngest of ten), with about four or five 'a-side'. On the paternal side were the McCulloch's and the Quinns, and Marion, Nancy's youngest sister, was named after her grandmother, Marion Quinn. On the maternal side were the Moodie's in the form of Alexander Moodie (Papa Sanny) and the Hamiltons. Nancy got the double whammy in name terms from her grandmother, Agnes Hogg Hamilton, while Trisha got the double benefit from being named Patricia Caroline, with Jeanette bringing up the Moodie line in her middle name.

Whilst the McCulloch family and descendents occupations were by no means exotic, there were some clear differences from the Rodgers. Papa Sanny was a 'locomotive driver' and there were public house keepers, police sergeant, stonemason, inspector of the poor, titles which were a bit more grand than the Rodgers. However, there was also a fair sprinkling of farmers, labourers, general servant, domestic, ploughman etc in the ancestry. In the main, the family hailed from Ayrshire, but with a strain from Caithness. Backtracking to the early 1800s reveals that the McCullochs originated in Ireland, with all but the Moodie roots being traced there.

Stone Cottage in Alloway is but a stone's throw from Burns Cottage and this is from where Nancy's great-grandmother sold ice-cream to the tourists who visited Burns Cottage. Whilst not quite sitting on a 'gold mine', the move to live with train driver Sanny certainly represented a 'crossing of the tracks' by moving to Barlieth in Hurlford.

After a week or two of 'going through the motions', in the aftermath of the wedding, there was a realisation that we did 'fancy' each other and we should 'go steady'.

If we were going steady, life for my Dad wasn't - he had a major heart attack and sitting with him in Ballochmyle Hospital, he was a 'pale imitation' of himself but even then, his sense of humour never left him – having no slippers, he fashioned a pair from the disposable urinals. Discharged from hospital after about ten days, he was steadily rehabilitated at work and I again helped out when I could – cutting grass here and digging a grave there.

Nancy worked full-time within the thriving lace manufacturing business in Darvel and with my money from the summer jobs, we could just about afford a four-day holiday in the 'Jewel of the Irish Sea', the Isle of Man. Memories of the Summerland fire had not completely cooled, but Jeanette and Janet McCann had secured jobs in a local hotel and we set off for a surprise visit, and our first holiday together. This holiday coincided with my first attempt to grow a beard and as I stepped onto the pier at Douglas, I looked like 'Shaggy' out of the 'Scooby Doo' cartoon.

We surprised Jeanette and Janet at the scene of the TT Races; the offshore dealings and the Casino night club helped us to express out freedom and our commitment to each other. The Isle of Man represented a poor man's hedonistic haven, as the yearnings of yesterday and the trials of tomorrow were set aside for living for today. It was an outward expression of our relaxed, cool and comfortable discovery of each other. We didn't strut, but felt secure and relaxed in each other's company. Friends began to perceive something more than friendship was at stake. Questions dipped and raised like a thermometer, as the question in our heads reverberated – *'Is he/she the one for me?'*

The strength of personal awareness and affection grew until on the top of the double-decker bus to Darvel, I declared,

'I love you, would you like to get engaged?'

It was not pre-prepared and there were no flowers or romantic music, but my offer was accepted. A Christmas engagement was too predictable, and 1st January was a much better time for a traditional Scottish celebration. So it was that on 'Hogmanay' 1979, we 'first-footed', 'second-footed' all the houses in Darvel with our relatives and friends, to show them 'the rings' after the 'bells'.

It was a frosty morning as we emerged from our sixth house of happiness. We trod warily down the stairs and avoided the treacherous pavements for the safety and sure-footedness of the main road. The *'carry-oot'* consisted of a bottle of Dry Martini and a full bottle of Black Rum, and a few cans of Tennents lager. Hand in hand, we gingerly walked to the next Hogmanay haven, when— I was down like a Saturday coupon! As glass went to tarmac, I was back up like a shot – *'Don't worry,'* says Nancy, *'it will be the Dry Martini.'* - no such luck and no Black Heart Rum for me, as the *'carry-oot'* bag, complete with the broken bottle, was deposited in the nearest bin. The event and embellished story, aligned to our engagement, got the sympathy vote and a good few drinks in compensation. People in equal measure were surprised and delighted for us. The declaration of our love made things easier and more relaxed in a social sense, but I had yet to graduate and secure a real job.

School and summer jobs had been in pretty plentiful supply in the 1970s. August on the Lanfine Estate, outside Darvel, was a time for the aristocracy to come and bag a few birds, in other words, shoot some grouse. Grouse beating, at £2 a day, was a good way to earn some money during the summer holidays. There was even a chance you would be walking the moors next to Robina, Lord and Lady Rotherwick's daughter. Lanfine Estate was owned by the Lord and Lady during the '70s, and the young Robina was a class act who everyone tried to follow and chat up, especially the older beaters. There was no danger of me pulling the lady, but there was distinct danger of being shot by some of the arrogant aristocrats, who had over indulged during the lunch-time break. The shooting butts resembled elevated First World War trenches and the shooters, with their Purdys and over and under shot guns, blasted both pheasant and peasant, as they flew or walked towards them

It was much safer to pick tomatoes during the summer and for three years, I tended tomato plants in their rows of three each side of the glasshouses, which seemed to run for about one hundred yards. Potato picking in September/October was also relatively safe at the Ireland's Bradley Farm, overlooking the tiny schoolhouse in which Sir Alexander Fleming's early education was nurtured, and at the Hamilton's Allanton Farm in the shadow of Loudounhill.

Whilst at Uni, any income earned during the summer holidays was tax free, and so a job that offered longer hours and more money was sought. Mitchell & Struthers, Sports ground Contractors of Kilmarnock, took me on. The job was ideal; the money was reasonable, it involved working outside, grass cutting, fencing and general groundwork, all over the South West and Central Scotland. It was a chance to earn some money and become more worldly-wise in the company of real workers.

Renovating gardens in Govan in the shadow of Ibrox Stadium, the home of Glasgow Rangers FC, was both daunting and delightful. Women actually did hang out of their windows, two stories up, and exchange conversation (and insults) with their neighbours, and throw their kids a 'jeely piece' out of the window. For a country boy who had gone to town, the city was a real eye-opener. At 3.00 p.m. midweek, three kids shuffled through a back court – the eldest, about seven, pushes a pram, whilst the second youngest, about five, carries an infant, about 12–24 months. Weird, I think, why is the baby not being wheeled about in the pram? Maybe there's another baby in the pram? As I try to peer in, the eldest troll advises – *'Fuck off mister'*. The baby is obviously lighter than the lead in the pram, which is being taken to the scrappy to convert into hard cash.

The money we earned as students was great and often I would leave Nancy's Mum and Dad's house to do overtime on a Sunday after a Saturday night out. Money draws greed and envy and when the real workers discovered we could earn as much if not more than them our basic wages were cut to £25 per week. Of the twelve or so students employed, only Hughie Williamson and myself were outraged enough to seek a meeting with management. We demanded, and got, a meeting with the MD, Ian Mitchell, and after a hard day's graft, we put our case to him. Either the force of our argument, or the fact that we were grubby urchins messing up his newly refurbished offices, won the day. In my first experience of potential industrial action, we secured a £10 'rise'. This was still lower than the basic rate for 'real workers', but true to the MD's word, the increase was paid to all the students and, with overtime, we still made good, tax-free money, with which I could at last pay some 'dig money' to my Mum and Dad.

Newmilns Vesevius 1974 Ayrshire Cup winning team, Backrow 'The Committee'

Middle row left to right: Drew Taylor (manager/coach), yours truly; John Guild, Rab Struthers, Bobby McNaught; Jackie Ferrie, Billy Fulton, Tony Wright, John McCreadie, John Sommerville (manager/coach). *Front row left to right:* George Fraser, Ian Allison, Ian McWatters, John Spence, Willie McMillan, Jimmy Finnie, Benny Ferrie and James McAllister.

Top: Myself in Torquay in the 1970s
Bottom: Nancy and I, 1980

Our Wedding

Top: 'The McCullochs' – (From left to right) Harry, Marion, Trisha, (myself), Nancy, Papa Sanny, Mavis and Jeanette

Bottom: 'The Rodgers' – (From left to right) Yvonne, Elaine, Avril, (Myself), Nancy, Mum, Dad, Lilian, Marlene, Davy, Bobby, Graham and Colin (Jim was ill).

CHAPTER THREE

'Times, and nappies, they are a changing'

Returning to Uni was traumatic, as an old order was re-engaged, and a new order was about to begin. But first, there was a question of completing my honours degree. Before graduating, I gained my first major title – not in sports or the honours list, but as President of Dalrymple Hall. I had been the dark-horse candidate but my nomination speech, advocating 'education, education and education' as my top three priorities, was well received, and well before it's time. However, even better received was my commitment to a mixed hockey team (some person in their wisdom had decreed that females could be residents of the Hall), video nights four times per term, and a Burns Night, complete with pipes and haggis-slayers. I lived up to my election promise as the hockey team was formed and was unbeaten in its Saturday morning outings, even against Queen Margaret Hall, complete with their three Indian and Pakistani exponents of the game, and the video nights, even if of dubious quality (The Texas Chainsaw Massacre and Blazing Saddles were big hits), were delivered.

The Burns Night was 'scary' – Jimmy Auld from Stewarton would address the haggis. Ronnie McGregor would deliver the toast to the lassies, and as the 'piece of resistance' I would remember the Immortal Memory. Tickets were sold and 'dignitaries' were invited. It was a sell out. The Hall was genuinely mixed, in terms of sex and ethnic origin and the dining hall was a riot of reds, yellows and greens, representing the African contingent; bright blues and whites for the Eastern entrants, and tartans for the Tuechters and Ayrshire entourage. The top table was formed as the Doc introduced us to the 'high-hied yins', who obviously had not encountered a Burns

Supper of this ilk – in fairness, they acquitted themselves well and did a fair bit of damage to the free wine and spirits at the top table.

A Burns Night without a piper is like a Juliet without a Romeo; a Morecambe without a Wise; a Stevie Wonder without a piano; an artist without an easel. At any rate, it was serious stuff when it was announced that the piper discovered he had a broken nose. 'Fuck me!' What will it take for him to play, short of a nose job? A half bottle tucked away in his Bearskin and our man did us proud. The drink flowed and the haggis flew – down people's throats. Everyone was up for it. Jimmy delivered the address to the haggis as if the postcode was missing and he slashed at the haggis as if to find it in its entrails. Ronnie brought all his charm and wit to woo the lassies – their reply would have made your ears prick – at least I think that's what she said. The Black Heart Rum gave me real heart as I delivered the 'Immortal Memory'. It would be good to think that in my Ayrshire accent, my delivery of the immortal memory was responsible for the warm reception, but in truth, it was the sense of occasion as a first, and the sense of the Bard's immortal truth, captured in 'To a Mouse', 'To a Louse', and 'For A' That & A' That'*.

---

* Poetry quoted is taken from, Douglas, W S (Ed.), *The Kilmarnock Edition of the Poetical works of Robert Burns*, Villafield Press, Bishopbriggs, 1938.

To a Mouse

***On turning her up in her nest, with the plough,
November 1785***

We, sleekit, cowran, tim'rous beastie,
O, what a panic's in thy breastie!
Thou need na start awa sae hasty,
               Wi' bickering brattle!
I wad be laith to rin an' chase thee,
               Wi' murd'ring pattle!

I'm truly sorry Man's dominion
Has broken Nature's social union,
An' justifies that ill opinion,
               Which makes thee startle,
At me, thy poor, earth-born companion,
               An' fellow-mortal!

          I doubt na, whyles, but thou may thieve;
What then? poor beastie, thou maun live!
A daimen-icker in a thrave
               'S a sma' request:
I'll get a blessing wi' the lave,
               An' never miss't!

          Thy wee-bit housie, too, in ruin!
It's silly wa's the win's are strewin!
An' naething, now, to big a new ane,
               O' foggage green!
An' bleak December's winds ensuin,
               Baith snell an' keen!

          Thou saw the fields laid bare an' wast,
An' weary Winter comin fast,

An' cozie here, beneath the blast,
            Thou thought to dwell,
Till crash! the cruel coulter past
            Out thro' thy cell.
That wee-bit heap o' leaves an' stibble,
Has cost thee monie a weary nibble!
Now thou's turn'd out, for a' thy trouble,
            But house or hald.
To thole the Winter's sleety dribble,
            An' cranreuch cauld!

But Mousie, thou art no thy-lane,
In proving foresight may be vain:
The best laid schemes o' Mice and Men,
Gang aft agley,
An' lea'e us nought but grief an' pain,
For promis'd joy!

            Still, thou art blest, compar'd wi' me!
The present only toucheth thee:
But Och! I backward cast my e'e,
            On prospects drear!
An' forward, tho' I canna see
            I guess an' fear!'

To a louse

Ha! whare ye gaun, ye crowlan ferlie!
Your impudence protects you sairly:
I canna say but ye strunt rarely,
                    Owre gawze and lace;
Tho' faith, I fear ye dine but sparely,
                    On sic a place.

            Ye ugly, creepan, blastet wonner,
Detested, sunn'd by saunt an' sinner,
How daur ye set your fit upon her,
                    Sae fine a Lady!
Gae somewhere else and seek you dinner
                    On some poor body.
Swith, in some beggar's haffet squattle;
There ye may creep, and sprawl, and sprattle,
Wi' ither kindred, jumping cattle,
                    In shoals and nations;
Whare horn nor bane ne'er daur unsettle,
                    Your thick plantations.

Now haud you there, ye're out o' sight,
Below the fatt'rels, snug and tight,
Na faith ye yet! ye'll no be right,
                    Till ye've got on it,
The very tapmost, towrin height
                    O' Miss's bonnet.

            My sooth! right bauld ye set your nose out,
As plump an' gray as onie grozet:
O for some rank, mercurial rozet,
Or fell, red smeddum,

I'd gie you sic a hearty dose o't,
          Wad dress your droddum!

          I wad na been surpriz'd to spy
You on an auld wife's flainen toy;
Or aiblins some bit duddie boy
          On's wylecoat;
But Miss's fine Lunardi, fye!
          How daur you do't?[1]
          O Jenny dinna toss your head,
An' set your beauties a' abread!
Ye little ken what cursed speed
          The blastie's makin!
Thae winks and finger-ends, I dread,
          Are notice takin!

          Oh wad some Pow'r the giftie gie us
To see oursels as others see us!
It wad frae monie a blunder free us
          An' foolish notion;
What airs in dress an' gait wad lea'e us,
          And ev'n Devotion!

---

[1] This is, by readers *gentle* and readers *simple*, acknowledged to be one of the most perfect little gems that ever human genius produced. One of its couplets has passed into proverb: - 'The best laid schemes o' Mice an' Men, gang aft agley.' Extract from 'The Kilmarnock Edition of the Poetical Works of Robert Burns' – special presentation edition – The Scottish 'Daily Express' Glasgow 1939.

For A' That and A' That[2]

Is there, for honest poverty,
That hangs his head, and a' that?
The coward-slave, we pass him by,
We dare be poor for a' that!
For a' that, and a' that;
Our toils obscure, and a' that;
The rank is but the guinea's stamp;
The man's the gowd for a' that.

What tho' on hamely fare we dine,
Wear hodden-gray, and a' that;

Gie fools their silks, and knaves their wine.
A man's a man for a' that.
For a' that, and ' that,
Their tinsel show, and a' that;
That honest man, tho' e'er sae poor,
Is King ' men for a' that.

Ye see yon birkie, ca'd a lord,
Wha struts, and stares, and a' that;

---

[2] Burns could make much of very humble subjects such as the *Dogs*, the *Pet-Yowe*, the *Mouse*, and the *Auld Mare*: here we have him descending for a theme, still lower in the scale of animal life. Lowly, even repulsive as the subject is, however, he has done it ample justice, and makes it point a moral if it does not adorn his page.
Extract from 'The Kilmarnock Edition of the Poetical Works of Robert Burns' – Special Presentation Edition – The Scottish 'Daily Express,' Glasgow, 1939

Tho' hundreds worship at his word,
   He's but a coof for a' that:
      For a' that, and a' that,
         His riband, star, and a' that,
      The man of independent mind,
         He looks and laughs at a' that.
A prince can mak a belted knight,
   A marquis, duke, and a' that;
But an honest man's aboon his might,
   Guid faith he mauna fa' that!
      For a' that, and a' that,
         Their dignities, and a' that,
      The pith o' sense, and pride ' worth,
         Are higher rank than a' that.

Then let us pray that come it may,
   As come it will for a' that,
That sense and worth, o'er a' the earth,
   May bear the gree, and a' that,
      For a' that and a' that,
         It's coming yet, for a' that,
            That man to man the warld o'er
               Shall brithers be for a'

that.

For Burns the ploughman and near-pauper, reward and real recognition came with his untimely death. From observation, on the simple Mouse and Louse, powerful and emotional truths emerge:-

   'The best laid plans of mice and men
   Gang aft agley.'

'Oh wad some Pow'r the giftie gie us,
To see oursels as others see us.'

For the culturally-deficient (like myself) it's hard to relate and equate Burns to the famous American author, John Updike, who translates the 1785 verse into a 21st century version – 'Entitled to a well connected Mouse (upon reading of the genetic closeness of mice and men)'. Burns is unique and universal so Updike's work is either a 'Tour de Force' or a 'Tour de Farce' – you chose?!

Burns was obviously a man before his time as an array of gurus, consultants and Human Resource professionals exclaim the virtues of 360° feedback through which individuals can obtain an all-round view of how others view their behaviours and actions from their perspective. Burns was way ahead of the game, but typically his insight and foresight proved in vain for him. 'For a' that and a' that', Burns knew that honesty, integrity, common sense and respect were the true stamps of worth in his fellow human beings. Undying and universal truths which didn't make him a prophet in his homeland but which elevated the ploughman to Poet – the National Bard.

The lines delivered slowly, like Braveheart Wallace on the field of battle, were received over-enthusiastically by some who didn't understand a word, but understood the occasion. The Burns Night spilled out to the next morning and the scoreboard next day read – Burns Night 300, Morning Lectures 0. True to Burns's tradition, in any language it had been an unqualified success. New and qualified however, was the name of the game; the passport to the world of work!

The more intense the studying was required, the more intense I became. With a view to the future and as a bit of an outlet, I took driving lessons in the vague hope that when I gained my first job, I would have a driving licence to enable me to drive the company car!! At £8.25 a time, BSM at Anniesland were not cheap but, even after twenty-two lessons and a prescription of Valium from the Uni doctor, I failed my first test. I had come within six inches of an articulated lorry turning right at traffic lights, as I attempted to drive straight through. I could hardly see the traffic lights, never mind the indicator on the lorry, which was way over the level of the Triumph Dolomite I was steering.

Having failed my driving test, I passed my finals. Not being naturally clever, a 2-1 (Second Class, Level One) honours degree was my own aim, but it was a Desmond Tutu (2-2) for me. Still, after what seemed like an eternal succession of exams, from 'O' levels onwards, this was like climbing Mount Everest, or at least Ben Nevis.

The allotted date for graduation was Independence Day (4th July) 1980, but through a combination of bad planning and bad luck, I ended up on my own. My Dad had had another heart attack and was not fit enough to attend, but my Mum was bursting with pride and Nancy would have gladly have been there, but it was a working day and we had no transport to get there and back. The graduation photos were good, but could not really make up for Mum, Dad and Nancy not being there. The moment and the occasion was gone, never to be recreated!?

Job application had followed job application, as the CV was circulated in the expectation of gaining some recognition for five years of study. Final interviews with Fords and the SSEB (Electricity Board) for graduate trainee positions in Personnel Management failed to get me on the first rung of the career ladder, and self doubt and recrimination crept in. I wasn't good enough; why had I bothered, there had been plenty of jobs in the mid 1970s, and I had wasted all this time and effort? Mum and Dad dipped deeper into their pockets as, in the absence of work, I found a place on the Post Graduate Diploma in Personnel Management at Strathclyde University. What was another year in education, it would be worthwhile.

Another year at Uni meant reliance on grant-funding (this effectively amounted to £9 per week to get by on). As usual financial and moral support was provided from Mum and Dad, Nancy and the family. *'Has your boy not got a job yet? I thought he was clever,'* was the type of comment that got me down, but not my Mum or Dad, not a word of it.

The Western SMT bus from Darvel to Kilmarnock, Kilmarnock to Glasgow, underground from Bridge Street to Buchanan Street, and a walk to the Strathclyde Uni buildings became the order of the day, every weekday, and every weekday, my Mum got up before me and made my breakfast. It was becoming too much and to the rescue came Jim McCaffrey, who knew some people who were looking for someone to share a flat – and the rent – with. A meeting of my potential flatmates was hastily convened. The Great George Street, top-floor flat (off Byres Road) was better placed for Glasgow University, but it was a hop, skip and a jump to the Byres Road (Hillhead) underground station and a world of a difference from a two-hour plus bus journey. The flat itself was spacious, with a bright green shag-pile carpet, which had been fashionable once – and once only! It now had the appearance of a huge, dead cat, with the shag well and truly knocked out of it. My potential flatmates were all vets (veterinary students) – maybe the carpet was made of dead cats after all! I had no problem with vets, but they were all female. I expected Nancy to be a bit wary, but pragmatic as ever, she had no problems with it and I joined the Great George Street Gang and slept in a sleeping bag until a bed could be procured for me in my single room.

After deductions for rent, gas and electricity, I had the princely sum of £9.00 a week to cover everything else – travel, books, clothes and food. It was lucky that denim (however faded) never went out of fashion, and even if it did, I never noticed. Cornflakes, bean sprouts, cabbage, beans, bread, smash potatoes, pizza, sardines and pork and liver became the main constituents of my diet.

Next to medicine, the veterinary degree is regarded as one of the hardest to get into and one of the hardest to pass. All five vets enjoyed a laugh and a drink but when the time for studying came round, they were focussed on their own personal ambitions and intent, and all succeeded in their 'finals'.

My diploma year fellow students were a mixed but likeable bunch and included pals, poseurs and pot-takers. The exams were completed and after a celebratory dinner, the Diploma team adjourned to the Strathclyde University Union Disco, to share memories, friendship and potential success in our exams. The evening was relaxed and cool, until wee Robert declared to big Frank and myself, *'That guy's jist punched me in the face and I've hurt my hand.'* The inevitable question followed: *'Whit did he dae that fur?'* *'Nothing,'* was the reply and I was off. *'Where is he?'* *'Over there, white shirt, by the big guy on the left.'* I followed Robert's directions to the letter and confronted the assailant – *'Don't know what you're talking about, now piss off before I....'* I got my retaliation in first, as Robert staggered over, surveyed the guy on the ground and says, *'That's no him, it's him,'* pointing to a six-foot bear of a guy. What the hell, to the strains of David Bowie's 'Life on Mars', all hell broke out on earth, as tables, chairs and glasses took to the air in an unreal and surreal fashion. The fatal combination of booze, birds and music had struck again. Later, Robert contemplated perhaps he was at fault in trying to pick up the 'big guy's' girl, as we emerged from casualty in the early hours of the morning, with confirmation he had broken his thumb.

The parcel said, *'Do Not Bend'* as my Diploma was delivered through the post in September 1981 – what a contrast to the formality of the occasion of graduation in Bute Hall at Glasgow University the previous year. The mail also delivered responses to applications for jobs and they were many and varied but most, although polite in tone, were labelled by me as GTFs (get tae fuck). GTF would have been a good name for a band but was definitely not good for my morale.

Back on the home and family front, the marital focus was on Bobby, Yvonne and myself.

Bobby had met Linda at the *'Covies'* (Covenanters Hotel in Newmilns – now somewhat symbolically a sheltered housing complex) and spent many a weekend at Sanquhar, where

Linda stayed. Sanquhar is home to the oldest Post Office in Britain, but it appears it was not the home of any 'first class males' as the girls of the town seemed to take flight and find their fiancés elsewhere. Their wedding was in Sanquhar and my Dad, following a major heart scare, had secured the doctor's permission to be released from hospital to attend the wedding. It was a long day for Dad, who had never seen so many of the family living it up on the bus home, while he felt like death.

In the meantime, Yvonne and Jimmy (he of the Mark 1 J registration Capri) were going steady and Nancy and I joined them on the heady days of 18th and 21st birthday parties, engagements and weddings, as life and love developed around and among us. Scarborough was 'revisited' and as Mr Rodgers and Nancy, we joined Jimmy and Yvonne and Tom and Ellen plus kids on our summer holidays. Mr Collins, married Jimmy and Yvonne on his home patch, Darvel Central Church, in August 1981.

Nancy and I set the 26th of September 1981 as the date for our wedding – we set if before realising Jim and Jessie had been married five years previously on exactly the same date. We were not (and are not) churchgoers and there would be no change in our approach to the wedding. The Community Centre in Hurlford was the venue (their first-ever ceremony on the premises), and the perennial pastor, Mr I Collins, conducted the service. It was a close family and friends wedding and even then, we mustered over 100 guests in attendance. My brother, Davy would be the best man and Jeanette, Avril and Marion were the bridesmaids.

Marion's photos as an eleven-year old Gala Queen, Hurlford's first, adorned the hall's walls in an uncanny link to both the past and the future.

It wasn't really a nervy day as we had had our ups and downs before I had secured a job as a Graduate Trainee with the South of Scotland Electricity Board (SSEB). This had taken the real pressure out of our relationship and ensured a more relaxed approach to the wedding celebrations. 'Pay off' and 'Stag night' celebrations had been enjoyed and this was it – a lifetime commitment and the biggest decision we would ever make in our lives. It was unequivocally the right decision.

The day was a fairly typical end of September day in Scotland, a bit windy, occasional showers with bright interludes. The weather forecast pretty much summed up the wedding but the bright interludes were larger and more enjoyable. True to form at a good Scottish wedding, as the bride and groom, we were reluctant to leave a good party in full swing. Still, it was our honeymoon and we really had to go.

We had to go to 4 Kirkland Road in Darvel, as our honeymoon retreat and home for the next few years. We had rented a one-bedroomed flat in Darvel and in the absence of winning the pools, this was as far as we got for our honeymoon. It wasn't something that bothered us; there was no envy and no regrets. There was also no peace, as in the early hours of the morning, the drunken guests on return from the wedding serenaded us after they found out we had honeymooned at home.

After three days honeymooning at home (not quite a la John and Yoko), we decided it would be safe to go out. Mr and Mrs Rodgers set off down the street, hand in hand, to get the messages and give everyone the message we were man and wife. Together, we faced the world, or at least, Darvel. Nancy's Mum and Dad, true to Scottish tradition, had paid for the wedding, and my Mum and Dad had given us £500 as a wedding gift and, practical as ever, we had spurned the honeymoon abroad for a fridge freezer.

Nancy returned to work and I began work with SSEB on the 12th October 1981. Still without a driving licence, never mind a car, it was back to a bus to Kilmarnock and the connecting bus to Glasgow and a walk to Cathcart House on the south-side of Glasgow, pretty near to Hampden Park, the scene of the 1973 successful encounter with Czechoslovakia and a few more since. Within a couple of weeks, this nightmare journey ended, as I secured a lift with Gordon and Danny, fellow workers at Cathcart House.

Our joint incomes as a Graduate Trainee and a Wire Cutter/Machinist within the textile manufacturing industry were not great, but we could still afford to go to the 'pictures'. 'The Champ', starring Jon Voigt and Ricky Schroder was one of the first and saddest films we saw. It was pretty run of the mill throughout, but the ending had me choking and in typical Scottish male fashion, holding back the emotion and tears, which desperately wanted to break free. *'Wake up, Champ, get up, wake up'* resonates in my head and have been my forlorn plea at two particular hospital bedsides since then.

As my training progressed, my salary increased and we became both more personally and financially secure. We took our landlord to a rent tribunal and his failure to respond or attend resulted in the rent being halved. At this rate, we could actually afford a holiday abroad and so eight of us struck out for Benalmadena near Marbella/Torremelinos on the Costa del Sol. The Maite Apartments were not plush but Puerto Banus seemed like a haven for bashful Brits in need of some sun and seclusion. Rolls Royces, expensive yachts and cruisers, male hands with gold rings which shone like knuckle dusters, and knuckle dusters which shone like rings. Puerto Banus was a place to be seen and watch another world and model girls go by.

The 'team' took to the Aqua Park outside of Torremelinos and without a drink in sight, climbed up the 200 steps to 'do a kamikaze'. Open gratings on the stairs left little to the imagination – we were up a helluva height and there was no going back down the stairs once you reached the top. *'Lie back, cross your legs at the ankles, cross your arms in front of your chest and ease yourself forward – whatever you do, don't sit up as you ease forward.'* Whoosh and oh shit – exhilarating, frightening, but repeatable – for some. Ronnie King though, had had enough, as he declared, *'Big Mags, I think I've shit myself.'* I don't think any of us would have 'done the Kamikaze' if they had told us there had been two fatalities in the previous years!

Our first holiday abroad had lived up to expectations and only the journey home remained. The flight from Malaga to Gatwick, rail journey to Euston Station and the connecting bus to Kilmarnock in Scotland. It was tight and delays with the flight left us to ponder what next, as we sat on our cases in Euston Station. Nothing else for it, we would sleep in the station and catch the first bus home in the morning. No problem – until I peer at my case and discover I've changed my name to Joe Wade – hell, I wish I'd picked a better name or better still, I wish I had picked up my own case at Gatwick. Perhaps Joe has my case, I think, as I phone the number on the address label. No such luck. Joe confirms, in a tone which indicates the insurance money was a better prospect than the return of his case full of 'manky' washing. At 2.00 a.m., I return Joe's case to Gatwick, in the vague hope my case is still there. Explaining the position to airport security, I am escorted to an area with ten or twelve unclaimed cases and lo and behold, Mr and Mrs Rodgers strike it lucky. Joe's case is exchanged for ours and I make to leave the area. *'Where are you going son?' 'I'm just leaving. 'You're not leaving without going through customs.' 'But there's no-one there.' 'It doesn't matter.'* So I pick green for go and I'm out of there and back to Euston in time to rejoin the team and get the 6.30 a.m. Stagecoach to Scotland. Thanks be to Brian Souter.

Eighteen months of graduate training and I'm ready for the real world of work in SSEB. Applying more in hope than expectation, I obtained my first post and Training & Welfare Officer at Cockenzie Power Station. The job offers a considerable rise in salary – only trouble is, it is in the 'far east' – in Preston Pans, just outside Edinburgh – a house move is in the offing.

Sam Downie, Driving Instructor, was the sign on top of the Ford Fiesta as I tried to enter the passenger seat. *'No,'* Sam says, *'it's actually better if you sit in the driver's seat to learn to drive.'*

The guy has obviously never heard of me and hasn't a clue that I can't drive. *'Don't despair, I'll get you there,'* should have been his motto, as I fail my test for the second time, by trying to drive down the right way of a one-way street, when everyone else is driving up the wrong way. I knew before the words were on the examiner's lips, that I'd just bagged a brace of failed tests.

In consolation on the way back, Sam suggests I join him in a marathon – *'Fuck me, I'm no having another twenty-six lessons.'* *'No, no, how would you like to run a marathon?'* I think – well at this fucking rate I've no chance of driving it, so what the hell? The Irvine Valley is to Holland what Dolly Parton is to Twiggy – there's some big hills out there! The training commences and ten or twelve miles, four nights a week is in the bank. My colleagues at work support the Edward Appeal, which is for a wee boy in Newmilns with cystic fibrosis. The training goes to plan and we're up to eighty miles a week - my driving lessons don't cover this mileage.

I sit with the same examiner who had failed me last time round and as he questions me on the Highway Code, I think, you must remember me, because I remember you, but I've done a helluva lot better since the last time. *'Mr Rodgers, I'm pleased to say you've passed your test!'* I resist the temptation to kiss the guy but Sam is ecstatic, or so it appears. Two weeks later, Sam takes a heart attack – I think it was his! Seriously, he offers me his sponsor money if I complete the marathon for me and him – I think, I'll never do fifty-two miles, but Sam reassures me that twenty-six miles will be enough and proceeds to give me directions on the marathon route – once a driving instructor, always a driving instructor!

Jim Richmond becomes my training companion and a one-off, twenty-two mile run (Darvel via Dungavel and return) with one bottle of water in just over three hours, gives me confidence I can complete. Dungavel (near Strathaven) was then an open prison, some twenty years on it's gates are closed as it controversially becomes a detention centre for refugees seeking sanctuary in Scotland.

A two-tone brown and cream Ford Fiesta 1.1l has been secured at Newmains' auction, courtesy of Alistair (my brother-in-law). It's an S reg and I'm well chuffed as the car has a low mileage and two careful owners. What a load of shite – the car must have smoked 120 cigarettes a day, as every winter's morning, it coughed it's guts out. Like a mad John Cleese, I took to giving it a damn good thrashing and returning indoors and then returning five minutes later for the brown bullet to spring into action.

Jim and myself reached the half-way point of the marathon (thirteen miles) in some one hour, forty minutes. We were going well, until we hit Bellahouston Park and I'm sure the Pope in his Pope Mobile would have passed me – I'd hit the wall. The advice to 'take plenty of fluid' had backfired on me, as the freezing water out of what seemed like the fifty-gallon 'oil drums' chilled my stomach. After stopping at the toilet at around twenty miles, I think, *'I don't remember drinking red cola?!'* – I decided to finish the job. People all through Glasgow were fantastic – you could have a drink, a sugar barley sweetie, tea on the back lawn or join the barbecue – like Japanese prisoners of war or Scots football fans in Argentina I think most of the runners have now returned from the first Glasgow marathon, but I could be proved wrong.

Three hours and some fifty minutes, and the journey was done, as I was greeted by Jeanette and Fiona (Nancy was at home, ill) and some tinfoil in which to baste myself later? Events of the day were relayed gleefully as I explained how I have very nearly run out of steam. Steam was the operative word, as it spewed from the bonnet of the wee car – it would have to go!! Never mind, the 'Edward Appeal' benefited to the tune of over £150.

Musselburgh (the 'Honest toun') is home to a racecourse, the pub once owned by Willie Ormond – that great Scotland national football manager; and the Brunton Theatre, and soon it was to be home to us. Six weeks in a hotel adjacent to the racecourse, a period of 'digs' in Tranent with Mrs McGowan, the wife of an ex-miner, were followed by the purchase of a one-bedroomed, terraced house at 17 Monktonhall Terrace, Musselburgh. At £22,500, we could have bought a three-bedroomed house in Darvel for that. Both sets of mums and Dads became worried and protective, as we set out to be really on our own.

The house was really a 'manse' in style and décor, as it had once been the home of a minister. The potential of the house was realised as we decorated during the summer and built a new fireplace and fitted new carpets in every room. After two months of bare floorboards and sleeping on an airbed, it was sheer luxury to walk barefoot on the new carpets and to sleep in our first new bed.

Help with the decorating had arrived in the shape of Marion, Davy (her boyfriend) and Jeanette. Davy was a gem, his character fitted his skin and he was very comfortable in it. He had no pretensions, he knew who he was and lived life as it was. He was big (even fat), bold, funny and straight, but had a gentleness and sensitivity which belied his size and outward confidence. He was also a bloody good football player and a 'teddy bear'.

Marion, by contrast, was petite (under five feet tall), quietly exuberant (bubbly), dedicated to caring for others, and 'incident-prone'. Kirklandside Hospital was her first challenge as to whether she could stick it as a 'carer' at the tender age of sixteen. Bed pans, bed sores and bed linen were all taken in her stride. Personal hygiene was next and the false teeth were collected for cleaning and returned to the 'gumsy' owners. No problem with the collection, but recognising who they belonged to in one big bag was a problem!! Hairdressing problems could also be solved, as the weekly visit by the hairdresser was curtailed due to illness. Wee Marion lifts the despair; no problem, a wash and the hair rollers in would set the old folks up fine. Curls turned to drooping ringlets as the awful truth dawned – she'd put the curlers in the wrong way round. Still, the old dears felt better for the hair wash and in the mirror they were the image of their mind's eye.

Help also arrived in the shape of Nancy's Dad, Harry and big Robbie, the joiner – their mission to complete a partition in the house to create another bedroom. We're short of plaster – board so I walk down to the wood merchants and fly back up the hill, wind assisted whilst carrying an eight by four sheet of plasterboard. The jobs done and for Harry and Robbie its time for them to get plastered themselves. We hit the Ship and then the bar once owned by Willie Ormand. Harry gets pretty merry early on and it's easy to see why and how his best days are behind him, and he's only about fifty. He is in fact like George Best today – haggard, drawn, wasting his talent and his liver, but Harry will have to make do with one liver. For now he's happy, argumentative and even arrogant with alcohol and he shares jokes with new found friends who stand Harry as he stands them a drink.

In our early twenties, life was for the living, and even the death of an older family relative did not dampen youthful spirit for long. At 6'4", and barely in his twenties, Danny McCann was a strapping big lad. At Chapel Hall discos, he would delight in saying, *'Hey big man, want to buy some raffle tickets?'* and he was talking to wee Kenny. He had a great sense of fun, fairness and football, but cancer, as in the case of countless others, did not respect his youth, geniality or genuineness. His face and body grew a shadow of their former selves; he strived to be the same Danny, but the 'tammy' on his bald chemotherapy head could not hide his and others fears. A period of hope called remission was short-lived as the revolutionary cancer treatment he was piloting produced hope for others but no miracle for him. He died on 19 November 1982, three months after his 21st birthday.

We'd never been to a funeral of someone so young and close enough to regard as a real friend. It was also the first catholic funeral I attended and the first time I have ever been in a chapel. The atmosphere was not an atmosphere, it was pure emotion. The priest slowly swings the thurible over Danny's coffin and incense does nothing that it is supposed to do: it does not help balance and clear the mind; it does not purify the air; it does not increase faith - it stinks – the whole fuckin thing stinks - Danny's DEAD! A 'celebration of life' in song and prayer and it was all too much for me. Past memories, Danny's family and the sight of the coffin culminated in a dam of tears being released like sluice gates – I had to get out of the chapel and, releasing my hand from Nancy's, I headed for the door before I made a 'fool' of myself. Out on the steps and in the fresh air, I was joined by other 'emotional fools' and we just nodded to each other, tears streaming down our faces in respect and reverence of 'Big Danny'. These tears and cries were not 'normal' (especially in Scottish men) but they were the most natural outpouring of grief and anguish and all the more painful for that.

Even in death, bigotry and sectarianism raised its head; *'That's one less papish bastard to worry about'* were the words reported back to me. The unbelievable was confirmed as being the undeniable. Ignore or confront was the question – confront when ready was the answer. Weeks passed before the day of reckoning, and even then, the bigot hadn't the guts to admit his words or real feelings. He was a typical coward; a 'big man' in the right company but a small-minded, squealing bigot when put to the challenge.

Bigots come in many shapes and sizes but only two colours – green and blue – one extreme is as bad as the other. Neither had a monopoly on religious hate and fervour but when combined, both should remember that blue and green make yellow. 'Old Firm' clashes (Celtic vs Rangers football matches) allow '90 minute bigots' to release their religious fervour and return to 'normality' as the heat and hate of the matches subdues. The whole social strata is reflected in this 90 minute bigotry – the poor, the rich, blue collar workers, white collar workers, the intelligent and the not so intelligent. They are all caught up in the history and histrionics of the game.

Bigotry it seems is bigger than patriotism as the majority of Celtic and Rangers cannot bring themselves to bear supporting the other team in their respective quests for success in the European field.

'In death there is life' is a sentiment both priests and ministers seem to share and essentially, 'life goes on' – not the same, but 'poorer for the passing' but richer for the relationship. So it was that Joanne came on the scene as the first and only of Nancy's nieces. Fiona and Ian had also got married and it was time for Tenerife. A walk down the Tenerife Main Street at 1.00 a.m. and we thought we were in the 'Caves of Drach', but no, this was 'Veronica's', a heaving, sweaty mass of flesh queuing and spewing for drink. Even in our early twenties, this was our one and only visit. The mission was accomplished when we found a good Sol Hotel with a great pool, free sunbeds and entertainment all day and night – we were in and to round it off, free dinner tickets were provided by a fellow Scot, whose son preferred to eat out on 'burgers'. Ah well, 'no loss what a friend gets'. Away from our own apartment we were residents at the Sol and even gave 'our room numbers' when we won prizes as part of the evening entertainment.

The major obstacle to getting up Mount Tiede (apart from the smell of sulphur) was the cable car. It swayed like a scene from a James Bond movie but it and Mount Tiede were conquered.

All too soon from Mount Tiede and the tempo of Tenerife we were back to the magic of Musselburgh and work at Cockenzie Power Station. In a bright July morning, the wee Fiesta, resplendent with new nearside headlamp, headed merrily from Tranent to the Power Station. A sweeping left hander past the Coal Plant and left onto the main road and I'd be set for a good early start. No such luck, as the coal dust, diesel and slight smirr of rain combine to pull me off the road onto the verge and through a small planting. The driver's door creaked open onto lush green grass. Through the undergrowth, I struggle to ensure the headlamp was still intact – yes, somebody up there likes me – and my car. No – as I peer back and discover, the underbelly of the car has been torn away by stones and tree stumps, and the passenger door has been 'panned in'. The car was no longer the star and for £850, I had secured a 'write off'. Never mind, we'd only paid £1,150 for it two years ago.

Amongst the managers at Cockenzie, Saabs seemed to be all the rage, so I took great delight in parking my borrowed racing bike between the two 'flying machines'. Wearing a suit and carrying a briefcase, whilst steering/riding a racing bike is not too difficult on the flat, or even going downhill, but it's hellish going up the hill to Tranent. It kept me fit and raised my 'street cred' with they guys at the Station to the extent I was invited to the football team trials. The guys had nothing to lose; if I was crap, they could kick the shit out of a manager; if I was any good, then I might get a game. Cockenzie vs Glasgow North Service Centre and we're playing well but can't get an opener, until up pops yours truly and fires a shot in from about twenty yards. I'm giving it 'laldy' and waiting for the initial celebrations to begin – they never really did – short of two pats on the back and two glares, which clearly stated, 'I am a lucky wee shite.' The pub is a great leveller – we'd won 2–0 and to a man, the guys came forward and congratulated me on a great goal – but the sense was almost, 'you're in the football team today, but the management team tomorrow'. It was 'distance' closed back then by personal friendship and good working relationships, enhanced by a drink or two at a social night out ten pin bowling and the likes.

Physical or geographic distance was also something that had never really been put between the family. Lilian and Duncan lived in Sandford, all of twelve miles away; Bobby and Linda in Dumfries, about sixty miles away; and Marlene and Frank about four miles away in Galston – that is, until they decided to go on an African safari – 'permanently'.

In 1982, the opportunities for welders like Frank were greater in Jo'berg and a whole new life beckoned for Marlene, Frank and a precocious twelve-year-old Lorraine. Recognition of this opportunity 'out of Galston' didn't hold back the maternal/paternal fears and tears as we gathered in Glasgow Central to say 'goodbye'. One by one (and we had mustered a fair contingent of the family), handshakes, hugs and kisses were exchanged and we were left at the platform, waving to shadows which might never return from the 'dark continent'.

Marlene, Frank and Lorraine work hard and settle in Standerton and adapt to a new style of life with a fair gathering of 'ex-pats' to visit and share a 'bria' (BBQ) over a weekend. Marlene is more faithful in writing than us and one of her 1985 exchanges reads:

'Hi there Kenny & Nancy,

Have you had any luck in selling you house?? It's a bit of a hassle waiting for someone to like it and put an offer in for it. But I do hope by now you have had some luck. We are really pleased that Kenny got promotion, its good that he is proving himself. Kenny you will be started your new job now so I hope it is all going well with you.

The weather is still warm and we have had plenty of rain usually late afternoon or evening. So our grass is growing like wildfire. We have settled in fine here and its great having a proper garden.

We really got a shock when we got a letter from Mum about Alistair's accident. But we keep hoping that things will work out all right for Alistair. Elaine must be taking it very hard as it's a strain trying to put a face on.

Lorraine got her braces out on Sat 2nd March so she is pleased as punch. Her teeth are lovely, nice and straight and white. I was supposed to be starting squash again after Xmas but would you believe we haven't started yet, keep putting it off.

About 9 months ago, don't know if you will remember or if I even said. But Lorraine got a cyst cut out of her cheek; well the damn thing grew back in as we had to take her up to a specialist up in Pretoria. So he cut if out again on the 6th March so she has still got the dressings on. She has to get the stitches out 12th March. So we are hoping it is done correctly this time. For seemingly with a cyst if you leave the slightest piece of lining it will just grow back in. Well at last Frank is getting plenty of overtime and kept very busy so that pleases him. So now we are going to save like hell and get some money in the bank.

We bought 2 tyres for the car and would you believe the bloody exhaust has a hole in it now. So that will be the next thing. I got a R50 fine about 2 maybe 3 months ago. Went down to Secunda with Lorraine and we had quite a bit of shopping so I told Lorraine to wait and I would get the car, so when I came round I drove in where the buses stop, picked Lorraine and shopping up, drove out and the bloody police were sitting; they had stopped a man who had done the same as me, went in a no entry sign. So he writes out the fine, asks me to sign it. I looks, saw R50 and said he must be joking, so he says 'Lady, I could fine you R100,' so I said okay, I'll take the R50, the B★★★★★d. Well, think that's all for so take care.

All our love, Marlene, Frank and Lorraine. xxx'

As if to say, 'Well you've had it pretty good for a while; let's test you out a bit further; let's see what you're made of,' life dealt an immediate crashing blow to Alistair and Elaine. The car crash was serious but dragged from the wreckage, Alistair would survive, that was not in doubt. How he would survive was in doubt, as confirmation came he was paralysed from the chest down.

The why Alistair? why Elaine? why us? questions were asked often but never answered, but Alistair and Elaine showed 'how'. With immense support from Elaine, Alistair literally took his life in his hands and developed skills and mobility that necessity demands, but nobody wants to have to master. The challenge is confronted, like the crash into the tree – head on. A one-bedroom flat with a two-year old Kevin growing up and demanding more of his Mum and Dad means a house move. A semi-detached house with lots of potential is bought and the potential is fully realised as Elaine, Alistair and Kevin turn it into a home designed to meet their needs. The wheel chair is mastered; as an ex-garage mechanic the car is re-engineered and fly-fishing is re-invented on a folding chair strapped to a rowing boat on the Lake O' Mentieth – the only lake in Scotland, and painting 'draws' Al closer to his latent talent. Independent, inspirational and included were Al's attributes and those which 'able-bodied' people would do well to aspire to. All this was only achievable through exceptional courage and application and support, without selfish pity or condescension, and after considerable nursing care in Phillipshill Hospital in East Kilbride, and the Victoria Infirmary in Glasgow.

After almost two years working/waiting, like corporation buses, three opportunities for promotion came along for me at the same time. I had offers of a promoted post at Cockenzie, a new one at the nuclear power station at Torness, and a return to Glasgow in Industrial Relations & Policy. The lure and lucre of the west proved too strong and our house in Musselburgh was sold at a £6,000 profit. The terraced house sold quickly but a purchase in the old home town didn't coincide with the sale. Lodging at 4 Kirkland Road, Darvel, was back on the cards, but this time, in ground left with Jeanette. The arrangement was to be that we would pay Jeanette's mortgage and she would return to stay with Mavis and Harry until we bought a new house. Mavis in particular had missed Jeanette, but had also gained another lodger in Davy, Marion's boyfriend. The happy family was recreated, with the exception of Harry. With four daughters, Harry found it harder and harder to be a man's man in a woman's household, and had been taking refuge in a bottle for some time. He was a man's man when it came to allotting housekeeping to Mavis from his wages as a Machine Operator with the Glacier Metal in Kilmarnock. He 'cheated on' his wife and family in a financial and emotional sense and it was becoming obvious to them all – he was losing it and them in a world where alcohol made him feel comfortable, and everyone else uncomfortable. 'Man to Man' talks with John and myself seemed to help for a while and then he would be off the rails and 'on the drink'. It was a demon everyone wanted him to conquer but events and circumstances conspired against Harry and sided with the demon.

Still, as long as Mavis had her daughters, she was strong enough to deal with her own job and Harry's shortcomings. Trisha and Nancy had left the nest and Jeanette returning temporarily only served to highlight Harry's hopeless fate. A return to her home to stay with us (after less than a fortnight!) was the only way to avoid some heavy personal clashes and confrontations, which Harry and for that matter, Mavis, were not ready for, as neither accepted reality – one drowned herself in her daughters and grandchildren, and the other just continued to drown himself in alcohol and self-delusion.

45 Anderson Drive in Darvel became our home after we had been 'gazumped' in the purchase of 38 Anderson Drive. In Scotland, it is relatively uncommon for an offer to be accepted on a house and then 'dropped' or withdrawn at the last minute, but our unhappiness with the situation was more than compensated by our move to our 'new' house. Settling back into the old home town provided better opportunities to catch up with old friends and relatives. Alexander Moodie (Papa Sanny) was one such relative. An ex-train driver who had amassed a wealth of railway experience and a range of general knowledge which would not have been disgraced on 'Mastermind'. Sunday afternoon visits were too quick but not before he had rattled through two chapters of an encyclopaedic mind. Long-term memory was no problem and the 1902 on the birth certificate was always quoted to account for short-term memory loss. Sanny's birth in 1902 had something to do with his physical frailty but it was his loss of mental prowess that was most obvious and disturbing. Mavis' efforts to cope with one 'invalid' was bad enough but as Sanny's dependency increased in proportion to his staggering memory loss, the

burden became too much for any one person to bear. Family, neighbours and friends would help, but this was Mavis' Dad, Nancy's grandad and he deserved the best effort and treatment to make his life worth living. A brilliant and vibrant mind offers no escape from Alzheimer's and so it was with Sanny. In his early stay in hospital, Sanny recognised this dreadful irony. In his last days, he didn't even recognise the hospital. Before then, he knew his fate and said his farewells well before he lapsed into a state of old-age infancy.

Degeneration and regeneration were walking hand in hand, as Sanny's life was eclipsing in June 1988, culture dawned on Glasgow. 'See Glesca, see culture?' and the Glasgow Garden Festival had sprung to life, as Sanny died at Crosshouse Hospital where wee Marion now worked, having 'served her time' with the elderly residents at Kirklandside Hospital. Having agreed to pick Trisha up at the Glasgow Garden Festival, I arrived in plenty of time to get back to Sanny's funeral. Carefully planned arrangements went out of the window as Trisha's coach had been re-routed to park on the other side of the Clyde from our rendezvous point. Frantic phoning came to nought, until the involvement of the police secured Trisha for the journey to the funeral. It was all too late – Sanny had had his send off by the time we arrived in Kilmarnock, but we joined the funeral party at the Foxbar and shared memories of Papa Sanny, before Alzheimer's destroyed his.

Nancy was twenty-seven and I was nearly thirty in 1986 – we would try and start a family – it wasn't just any family we wanted to start, but one of our own. A summer holiday in Gran Canaria was to be our last child-free holiday abroad for a wee while as Nancy's pregnancy was confirmed. From being a relaxing preparation for the new birth, the holiday in Gran Canaria became a real trial as unexplained and undetermined bleeding appeared to be heading for a miscarriage in the early weeks of the pregnancy. Countless couples had probably experienced the same or worse run up to a birth than us, but there is no substitute in terms of emotional involvement from 'being there'.

As Nancy's pregnancy developed, so too did the textile workers' dispute with their employers. As inevitable as a birth was on the cards, so too was an industrial dispute. The pickets and braziers were out. It had taken a long time in coming but it would take a shorter time in going – the days of lace and textile manufacturing in Darvel were surely numbered. It was another case of having to be there and do it.

'Being there' was an easy question for me to answer about the birth of our first child – the answer was simple – if Nancy wanted me to be there, I would be – but preferably with a seat in the balcony rather than the stalls. Maybe, just maybe, our first son would be born on Epiphany 1987 (thirty years after me) but warm and protected in Nancy's womb, he chose to stay beyond his estimated time and was getting close to the stage when 'jump leads' would have to be applied before he decided 'today's the day, I'm out of here!'

An early morning dash to Irvine Central Hospital got me there in plenty of time. Nancy was 'comfortable' – I don't quite know how this could have been, as an eight-pound baby was trying to make his way into the world with no conception of the pain this was undoubtedly causing. Holding Nancy's hand and encouraging her 'at the top end', the pains of labour became all too evident as sweat and pain etched across a normally faultless face. It was hard labour and pethadene was required to ease the pain and the birth, which was announced by our son being shot out at force down the blue, shiny mat for the midwife to catch, cradle and check, before quickly settling with it's Mum and me – it's a boy at 10.12 a.m. on Tuesday, 22 January 1987.

The pain of birth is too joyful for tears, as I phoned round the family and told them the good news. Grandparents first and then getting as many of the family in as I can. Having been the bearer of good tidings and with Nancy and the baby asleep, I sit with my bar lunch in the Redburn Hotel just opposite the maternity hospital. The scampi and chips suddenly appear to be in danger of getting soggy, as tears inexplicably start to trickle and eventually roll down my face. I peer to the bar to see if anyone has noticed me and decide who cares? I'm here, I'm proud – I'm a DAD! I actually want to proclaim this now but settle for tears being replaced by smiles and laughter. The bar staff were used to being next to the maternity hospital and smiled knowingly, as I gladly paid the bill for the soggiest meal I'd ever had.

A couple of days at Irvine Central and two more at the Kilmarnock Maternity Home, and then we are handed complete responsibility for our first son. His room is prepared, his cot is prepared, his nappies and clothes are all prepared. Are we prepared? No chance – this is a baby with a mind of its own which preys on your own mind. The carrycot becomes his bed next to ours and to avoid every parent's nightmare, he is checked every two hours (or more) 'to see if he's breathing'. He is breathing all right – only problem is he wants 'to be up and about' when we need to sleep. Gary's, or more accurately, Kenneth Gary's nocturnal activities, together with the desire to prove breast-fed is best are hard for first-time parents to come to terms with, but it helps us lose weight and to be able to fall asleep at the drop of a nappy!

Ten months into the 'survival course' we decide a break in Majorca would be 'nice'. Arenal in October was great. The Mallorcans took to Gary, or 'Gari' as if he was one of their own and for the first time, he slept when he should and took his bottle.

As Gary progressed from carrycot to cot and breast to bottle, Nancy could go back to work in the afternoons/evenings. Mavis could help out and this would keep her busy and help her from wondering and worrying about Harry. Harry, in his own mind and world is still going strong; he's got plenty of friends, helps his family and he's got a good job – what's the problem?!

As Nancy starts back to work, we share the work and I come home to feed, bath and bed Gary. This often ends up with me sleeping on the floor with one hand on Gary's back through the bars of the cot. Returning from work, Nancy awakens me and we try some adult conversation. The doctors assure us it is cyclical sickness as Gary throws up every day, day in day out for months and carpets and tempers get frayed with unending vomit. Eventually, the day in, day out cycle of sickness stops – after we've renewed the bedroom, living room and hall carpets. A holiday at St Anne's, outside Blackpool, does enough to reassure our faith in human nature, and we'd let nature take its course again – and try to add to the family again.

At this time and at St Anne's, an old association with Leeds (remember Killie v Leeds in 1967) reacquaints itself as we meet and enjoy the company of the Bullers family, from Morley in Leeds. Robert and Jill and family, in the form of Gavin, Shane, Katie and Sofie, combine with us to make a double family holiday.

Their family in a sense is everything that we are not – they're English, artistic and musical, but we share a drink, a laugh, kids' stories and kids playing, and a lasting relationship and friendship is formed.

Rebirth or at least renewal or retirement is on my Mum and Dads minds as my Dad agrees to have a retirement party in the Darvel Junior's Social Club on Friday 19 May 1989. After over forty years' service with 'the Council', the powers that be (Kilmarnock & Loudoun District Council) decided to honour this service with a small presentation to mark this occasion and that of some other 'worthies'. Service and recognition knows no bounds as they present my Dad with a 5' x 3' ceramic squirrel – nuts or what?! The expectation had not been out of this world – the reality was certainly within it – it was desultory, bordering on demeaning. How many of KLDC's managers and 'high heid yins' picked up the same ceramic squirrel for over forty years service – but these guys were only 'common workers!' Mum and Dad were visibly hurt by the totally inept attempt to mark an occasion, which they had looked forward to with 'old-fashioned' pride. True to form, my Dad laughed it off, although the squirrel would not take pride of place in the display cabinet – we would find a corner for it and it would be cheap and easy to keep.

Nancy's second pregnancy is coming along just fine and, as 'old-stagers' we are more relaxed and comfortable in the approach to the second birth. Gary is content to know he will have a wee brother or sister soon. May 1989 is hot (unusually hot for Scotland) as we pad up and down the grounds of Irvine Central Maternity Hospital. 'Nothing' is happening, as I think of leaving for home, only to discover we've got some 'movement'. The nurse is advised that contractions appear to be coming pretty steady now, but the nurse knows best, there's no hurry as the nurse tells Nancy – *'You haven't got a labour face.'* An hour later and I've had a Tory, Liberal Democrat, SNP and back to a Labour face as no-one has been near for an hour, and Nancy definitely knows things have well and truly started. I hotfoot it in search of the midwife, who then casually checks Nancy and declares 'full dilation' and we're off in the wheelchair to the maternity unit delivery suite. The labour is shorter but the delivery is longer, as this baby decides to meander slowly out into the world. There is no explosion of a black haired baby onto the blue mat, only an inexorable entry which tears at Nancy and turns to tears of joy, as the wee fellow is out. He's out, but not using his lungs like Gary; he's a bit blue and a tube is quickly inserted into his mouth and mucus drawn out by the midwife sucking on the vacuum as if she needed petrol to get home that night. The 'gunge' is removed and the wee fellow and us breathe easily. Greg Alexander Rodgers is officially in this world at 12.53 a.m. on Wednesday 24th May 1989. He's a contented baby and we're home inside four days to be the new family.

The new and extended family is also extending directly in the McCulloch branch, as the 'live-in lodger' and Marion decide to take up and make a home of their own. Hurlford Kirk is the scene of the wedding as the Reverend Brodie marries Marion and Davy, resplendent in his kilt, on 5th August 1989. We have a great day back at the Parakeet and Harry copes well in his youngest daughter's greatest day. He and Mavis can really dance and this masks ongoing uncertainty and uneasiness, which is never far from the surface. The younger entourage, Joanne, Gavin and Gary all have a ball as, like mini magnets, they draw attention and money in equal measures.

The youngest of the immediate Rodgers' family was also drawing attention to himself, as Mum phoned in panic, despair and desperation, to declare, *'You can't go down the street today!'* Expecting the death of my Dad, or some near and dear relative, the explanation was offered – Graham smashed the chemist's window last night. In a family of 'no angels', but no trouble, Graham's breaking of the chemist's window in a fit of emotional and drunken rage was the 'low-light' of our brushes with the law. It was literally a sobering experience for Graham as he's never drunk alcohol since then. Apart from Bobby and me 'being reported' for eating Mrs Clark's daffodils on return from a good night out, there were no assaults, no robberies, no muggings down to a Rodgers. This was no consolation, as Mum couldn't face the street. It wasn't as if Graham had smashed the chemist's window to get at some prescription drugs – it was simply the fact he had done something patently and publicly wrong, which would be down to a 'Rodgers'. To Mum, everything that had gone before, in terms of 'good' had been undone with the first crack on the window. High standards, in expectation of common-sense behaviour were breached, and so visibly, so Mum's reaction was understandable – it was only a window, but it was Mum's window on the world, through which the Rodgers' were viewed – the image and reality were now cracked.

As if to repair the crack, I set off down the street – a bit self-conscious, but conscious that the absence of any Rodgers would be tantamount to disgrace and denial. Short-term disgrace it might have been, but there was no denial, least from Graham, as he pled guilty at Kilmarnock Sheriff Court, and was fined £400 plus costs. Being there with Graham, I felt this was harsh for a first offence, to a boy who was genuinely 'good'. The 'object of his emotion' was Elaine (Wee Elaine, even wee'er than our sister, Elaine). In an attempt to help Elaine's family taxi business, Graham took on some of the reception/call duties into the early hours of the morning. As a golf course greenkeeper, he was up early anyway and this soon caused friction with his employers, Loudoun Gowf Club (the only Gowf Club in the world, and in the spirit of reconciliation, well worth a visit). It was a short course, then run by short-minded people with short memories to match, who had forgotten why they had recruited Graham as their first YTS trainee greenkeeper and how he had turned out regularly and diligently to prepare the course and greens before the early-morning competition started. Refusal to work overtime on the level and extent previously worked was considered as a breach of contract and dismissal followed.

I take on the case for Graham. A late offer of £400 in settlement of the case was rejected and it was all or nothing at the Industrial Tribunal. I was up for it and we went through the details of likely question, responses and outcomes. All this went for nought, as Gary took ill and was admitted to hospital with suspected pneumonia. We're at the hospital until 2.00 a.m. and leave when he is deemed to be 'okay'. 6.00 a.m. and I'm back up to have an early start and get to the IT in Glasgow in good time. We're there in good time, but there is no good time. Less than four hours sleep kicks in early as I miss a golden opportunity to have the IT delayed, based on the fact that one of the IT (board/members) is declared to be the President of another Golf Club. Damned if you object and damned if you don't. I opt to go ahead and lose.

The report in the *Glasgow Herald* of course reflected none of the above in its 'Greenkeeper loses appeal over sacking'[*].

A Golf Club greenkeeper who was sacked after refusing to work at weekends during the competition season has lost his claim that he was unfairly dismissed.

Mr Graham Rodgers was dismissed from his job at Loudoun Gowf Club, Galston, Ayrshire, last November after twice having refused written requests to give an undertaking that he would work overtime during the 1991 season.

Mr Rodgers, of Muir Drive, Darvel, Ayrshire, maintained he could not be compelled to work overtime as it was not a condition of his contract of employment.

Although he had previously worked at weekends, he claimed this had been on a voluntary basis. At no time had he been told that there would be compulsory overtime to be worked.

Mr Rodgers had started work with the club in 1985 as an employment trainee, eventually being offered a full-time post as an apprentice and qualifying as a full skilled greenkeeper.

An industrial tribunal in Glasgow heard that last summer he told the head greenkeeper he was no longer prepared to do weekend work because of personal circumstances.

When interviewed by club committee members, he explained that he had to work for his girlfriend's father at the weekends due to a family crisis.

In an effort to resolve the matter, the club then wrote to him seeking written confirmation that he would be available and willing to do weekend overtime in 1991. He refused to give such an undertaking.

A second letter from the club, this time making it clear that refusal or inability to give the assurance sought could lead to dismissal, was met with a similar response by the greenkeeper, who was then dismissed.

Rejecting Mr Rodgers claim that his dismissal was unfair, the tribunal said it was satisfied that there was a requirement on golf clubs to carry out work on the greens on the days when competitions took place.'

---

[*] Extract from, 'Greenkeeper loses appeal over sacking', *Glasgow Herald*, 4th June 1991, page 7 – Home News.

It's the end of Graham's employment with the Gowf Club – not on his ability to perform his duties – he was bloody good at his job – but 'the Committee's' inability to allow a reasonable time for a young boy to get his life together. It was the end of a job, but not the end of the world. It was serious, but not tragic.

Serious but not tragic also applied to Gavin's accident. Like most local authority 'swing parks' in the 1980s and 1990s, the 'swings', roundabout, rocking horse and 'chute' were all mounted on tarmac or concrete bases and surrounds. These were hardly the most children-friendly surfaces in the event of the likely fall. The young Gavin had such a fall from the chute, but undeterred he continues as normal. Normal, that is, until his behaviour becomes abnormal – he is listless, has a sore head, and completely uninterested in everything. The doctor declares Gavin to be OK. Unconvinced, Trisha and John observe until they are stirred to action in face of telltale signs which spell 'danger ahead'. The incident escalates to emergency surgery to relieve the pressure on his brain which has resulted from his fall. A young Gavin awakes, with swollen eyes and an eight-inch red ridge and stitches curving round the left side of his head. The red ridge in time will subdue to an unbroken white line but the six-inch permanent scar in his head is infinitely better than a temporary six-foot scar on the ground to mark his grave. Only Trisha and John's insistence that Gavin was 'not right' and the skill of the surgeons at the Southern General saved the serious from becoming the tragic.

Top: My graduation. MA (Hons) Modern History and
Economics – 4th July 1980, Glasgow University

Top: Monkton Hall Terrace, Musselburgh – No. 17 is the
lower level house with the street lamp next to it.
Bottom left: Davy decorating No.17.
Bottom right: Marion decorating No.17.

Top: Gary and Greg on Holiday in SA Coma, Majorca.
Bottom: Laughing boy Greg.

CHAPTER FOUR

'A Trio of Tragedies'

Personnel Manager, Ayrshire District, became my title, as I move to Kilmarnock as my new employment base with SSEB. Newly rescrubbed and presented, the essentially public service becomes privatised as Scottish Power. A district of just over three hundred employees and probably with over three hundred relatives, was a great place to be. In the 'economies of scale' Vs 'small is beautiful' debate, the 'small is beautiful' won. Ayrshire is the District to be. The Team gel under John Menzies and Greenholm Street in Kilmarnock becomes the customer service centre for Ayrshire, as we win the first ever Ayrshire Quality Association Award.

Alex Kennedy, Joe Burns, Walter Russell, Les Burns, Jim Johnson, Ken Allan, John Menzies and myself become the first team. The Social & Recreation Club for Ayrshire blossoms, as John and myself do a karaoke cover of *'I've never felt more like singin' the blues'*, and everyone else covers their ears. Seeing was believing, but hearing was painful.

Jobs were also available within Ayrshire District and my brother Colin secured a fixed-term position as a General Duties Assistant (GDA), which, through his own efforts and application, is confirmed as permanent after six months. Marion's Davy meantime decides (at the age of almost twenty-four) he is too old to still be a milk boy and there's not enough money in it to pay the rent. An HGV licence would be useful to secure a job so Davy pays the course and exam fee with money borrowed from Nancy's Mum, Mavis, whilst still living with her and passes first time. Some short-term lorry driving work proves this driving about all day and night is not what it's cracked up to be, or at least, not for Davy on short-term contracts with employers who paid only what they could get away with. An 'anonymous' interview with Scottish Power results in Davy also securing a job at Kilmarnock, based on his own merits.

In the midst of all the relative contentment, Mum and Dad face up to the inevitable – the older they got the more difficult it was for them to continue to live at Hillcrest. Their home since 1959 would become someone else's house. 44 Glen Crescent in downtown Darvel was the address on all the gear, and Davy Clements, brother Davy, Colin and me get all the belongings down to the new house before Christmas 1992. Well into retirement age, this is an absolute wrench, but also an absolute must for Mum and Dad to be able to get out and about and for us to ensure everything is OK. Physically and mentally shattered from the exertions of the move, the early days at Glen Crescent seem a bit of a trial, but familiarity breeds contentment and a growing realisation that the good days at Hillcrest were 'banked' as carefully as Dad's weekly wages had been for over forty years. Grieving for Hillcrest was short-lived and living for Glen Crescent took off.

Normal working day follows normal working day, as the pattern of life begins to be beaten out at a more even rhythm. There are no huge upheavals, things and family are coming together. Small but very significant things happen – these are normal, happy, family things – Gary learns to walk and talk; Gary goes to Nursery School. Greg learns to walk and talk and thinks he should go to Nursery School with Gary. Nancy and I decide that the two Gs are enough family for us and I 'get the snip'.

Friday 8 May 1992. After overcoming my mental block and the painful reports from fellow 'snippets' or 'snippees' I am stripped and ready for action – at Ballochmyle Hospital. The action starts and could have ended with a quick shave but the nursing assistant has a keen eye, and a very steady hand, which is more than can be said for me. The action continues with a quick needle jab to the right testicle area and things are feeling well – pretty numb – that is, until the doc decides to make the incision, cut the tubes and tie a knot in them.

'Relax, you seem a bit tense,' was the nurse's observation – too right I was! But then, there are a helluvalot more painful things than a vasectomy; torn ligaments, leg breaks, childbirth etc and after a day or two and three or four baths, 'all's swell' becomes 'all's well'.

Physical pain, in whatever guise, cannot compare with the impact and long-lasting effect of emotional pain and loss. It had been a wee while since life had given us a kick in the teeth to remind us not to take it for granted and to value each and every moment. As if a 'wake-up call' were needed for the family, we were delivered not one but three blows – a kick to the stomach, one to the head, and then, when we were down, another one to the head. A trio of tragedies awaited us and there was not a thing we could do but live through it and in spite of it. It was something Marlene had to go through with Lorraine at a distance, when her Frank was killed in a road traffic accident in South Africa. At least we were at home and could comfort each other.

Like many 'ex-pats' Marlene and Frank had worked hard and made good since his first job as a welder in South Africa. The Scottish work ethic provided a base for progression to management and then to self-employment and a business to run. The lifestyle developed in line and holidays to Swaziland and a new house and the purchase of land followed. Triumph precedes disaster as Frank's pick-up leaves the road on the journey home and he is killed. Throughout the years since the early 1980s in South Africa, Frank had returned on a few occasions, including the death of his mother – but in his death, his brothers, sisters family and friends could not return their respect to him – Marlene and Lorraine had to shoulder this on their own as telephone calls were no substitute for a mother's embrace and a family's empathy.

By late March 1993, Davy and Marion were well settled into their new house in Hurlford – it's been redecorated and friends and relatives had all been round to help with the 'house-warming'. Two days of unabated sickness and diarrhoea are originally put down to a carry out meal on the Friday evening, but by Sunday afternoon the suspected food poisoning becomes a suspected obstruction and Davy is admitted to Crosshouse Hospital.

The following extracts from the twenty-six pages of Ayrshire & Arran nursing notes summarise Davy's medical conditions and treatments.

5/4/93

13.00 hours – *Emergency transfer via 4a at 10.45 a.m., with history of? food poisoning/nausea vomiting and loose foul smelling stools. Relatives spoken to by Dr Kidd.*

15.15 hours – *intubated and ventilated*

21.00 hours – *patient stable but ill.*

Nursing care – all care as tolerated, eyes clean, mouth dry, pressure areas intact. Family in attendance throughout the day – wife staying in Short Stay tonight.

6/4/93

Night report – very unstable throughout the night.

Sweating profusely, salivating + + + + + + + +

Nursing care – bed bathed, incontinent of faecal fluid x 4 overnight.

Condition deteriorated 5.00 a.m. Blood pressure down, no urinary output, peripherally shutdown. Seen by Dr Wilson, renal physician and Mr Paterson, theatre originally planned but patient not stable enough.

13.30 hours – *stable but ill.*

Seen by Mr Livingston and Dr McKay. Family in attendance.

6/4/93

8.30 p.m. *– In theatre 5.30 p.m. – 6.45 p.m. for laparotomy; division of (Mr Livingston and Mr Shetty) adhesions and release of obstructive loop of terminal ileum (?approx 2-3 litres of faecal fluid drained from gut under decompression).*

Air entry fair – harsh and duller to bases. No aspirate from chest.

Given extra fluid during theatre.

Nursing Care – now on air fluidised Clinitron bed. All care given as conditions allowed. Family spoken to by Dr Pary and have visited.

7/4/93

Inaccurate Swan Ganz reading

Care – bathed, shaved, central and arterial sites re-dressed, eye and mouth care, 2-hourly. Eyes remain oedematous. Wife and sister visited, prior to staying overnight in Short Stay.

1.30 p.m. *– Steady tho' slow improvement maintained.*

Nursing care – Abdominal wound redressed, wound satisfactory, abdomen less distended. Blood-stained … secretions continue to 'ooze' from nasal passages and mouth when disturbed. Mouth moist, tongue slightly coated. Wife spoken to by Dr Miller.

7/4/93

Generally stable.

Nursing care – All care 2° eyes remain oedematous mouth moist saliva and bile from op +++ pressure areas intact. Family in attendance throughout evening.

8/4/93

a.m. – Condition fairly stable overnight.

Nursing – Bathed this morning. Pressure areas satisfactory. Skin looks quite red, not hot to touch. Eyes remain very sore care given. Abdominal wound cleaned. Suture line left exposed, clean and dry. Light at times, settles well with sedation.

Generally stable but ill.

Ventilation – patient making effort (to breathe) but not moving volume.

Output – Nasogastric tube not in correct place as bile leaking from mouth and nose. Repositioned and 1,000 mls bile in suction container (on low suction).

Nursing care – Bed bathed. Pressure areas intact. Turned hourly. Eyes clean, mouth now clean and moist. No further twitching or seizures. Wife spoken to by Dr Wilson. Family visited this afternoon/evening.

9/4/93

a.m. – remains ill. Making very little respiratory effort overnight.

Neuro – Frequent twitching of trunk and upper limbs overnight. Extending both arms during seizures, tho' flexing arms to pain. Lower limbs flexing to pain – no response. Pupils are unequal – right size 4mm, left size 5mm. Very sluggish reaction to light. Nursing care – bed bathed. Mother phoned this am.

14.00 hours - Remains unwell but stable. CT scan shows cerebral oedema. To be fully ventilated to keep PaCo, 30. CMV FcO^2 increased to 70% post physio, as he desaturated to 86%.

Neuro – Left pupil slightly larger than right, reacting very sluggishly. Withdraws from painful stimuli 0800.

Sedated and paralysed now and for CT scan. Was still 'twitching' prior to this.

Nursing care – Wife and family spoken to by Dr Hildebrand re CT scan, also visited this morning.

***21.00 hours** – Condition still poor but very stable.*

Nursing care – Wife says she sees 'a big improvement in his appearance'. Relatives in attendance almost constantly, obviously very upset and asking lots of questions and needing information repeated several times. Neuro obs discontinued as he is sedated and paralysed. Pupils – right size 4 and very sluggish, left size 5 – very difficult to tell if pupils are reacting at al. Abdominal wound redressed. Bed-bathed and shaved.

10/4/93

General condition remains very ill.

Neuro – Pupils only size 2. Unable to detect any reaction.

Care – Bathed, shaved, pressure areas clean and intact. Eye and mouth care as charted. Visited by family. Relatives staying overnight in Short Stay.

***13.30 hours** – Condition stable tho' chest condition not improving.*

Nursing care – Pupils small and don't appear to be reacting.

***8.00 p.m.** – Condition unchanged.*

Nursing care – Bed-bathed, turned hourly. Eyes satisfactory now, mouth moist – tongue slightly coated. Light and making insp effort in afternoon, since sedation turned up, now more settled. Pupils remain small, reacting. Visited by family.

11/4/93

***6.00 a.m.** – Condition static*

Nursing care – Bed-bathed. Mouth dry, eyes as before, all care 2-hourly. Pupils pin-point, difficult to ascertain whether light reactive or not.

13.30 hours *– Sedation off from 07.45 a.m., Making respiratory effort.*

Output – One episode of rectal 'bleeding' – query collection from siggy (colon) biopsy, seen by Mr Sugden – just observe meantime.

Nursing care – Air fluidised Clinitron, nursed side to side. Eyes still puffy, dirty oral secretions. No response to painful stimuli. Wife, sisters and parents visited. Very distressed that he has not woke up and quizzing everyone. **Will need to be spoken to re overdoing visiting. Wife is still in residence in Short Stay ward.**

6.00 p.m. *(Dopamine) increased to 10mls with no effect. Patient not breathing at all. Unofficial brain death tests carried out with no responses. Family spoken to by Dr Miller, very distraught. Condition deteriorating quite rapidly.*

9.00 p.m. *– Condition very poor but stable at time of report.*

Post rectal bleeding, copious amounts fresh/serous blood before 5.00 p.m. 300mls–500mls. One episode following 5.00 p.m. 300mls in suction line. Pressure area care carried out each time.

Mother and father gone home. Brother has gone home. Wife and other relatives staying in Short Stay.

12/4/93

6 00 a.m. *– Very slow deterioration overnight. Members of family with David throughout the night. Nursing care – Bed bathed and shaved. All care provided. Support provided for all family members, appear aware of David's imminent demise.*

Neuro – Pupils fixed, dilated. No response to painful stimuli or otherwise.

Continues to deteriorate.

Neuro – Brain stem death tests carried out by Dr White and Dr Young. No response. To be repeated at 9.00 a.m. tomorrow. Family spoken to at length by Dr White and myself.

Nursing care – All care given as required. Support given to relatives.

Family present – support given.

13/4/93

4.45 a.m. *– Ventilation unchanged, as directed. Blood pressure slowly deteriorated further. Heart rate slowly falling, ECG becoming ischaemic, rate below 60, became asystole at 5.00 a.m., thereafter certified dead by Dr Cunningham. David's wife and other members of family present. All supported and comforted as much as possible.*

Without the aid of these medical notes at that time, we try to make sense of it all and to us, it seems by Monday afternoon, Davy is really struggling to breathe, and is put on a ventilator and lapses into unconsciousness, before we all get to see him and are told how serious he is. He has septicaemia.

Davy fights for his life in a silent struggle that is only broken by our pleas to wake up and letting him know how things are going outwith the hospital. Day in, day out, we try and have someone there for him to speak to and wake up to. Life support machines function for Davy as he ceases to function; he's with us in body but doctors decide they need to check if he's still with us in mind, after confirming that he has suffered from 'toxic shock'. This is a rare condition overall and even rarer for a male of Davy's age, twenty-eight years old, but it seems to have emanated from adhesions related to an appendix operation (some six years earlier).

Davy is operated on at Tuesday teatime to remove/repair the obstruction, and things are looking a bit better. By Wednesday evening, Jeanette, Nancy and Trisha are in better spirits as they clean their house a bit, changing the bed etc, in preparation for Davy being released, but Marion has 'a bad feeling about all this', which Mavis tells her is because she is feeling low and run down – Marion doesn't really believe her. By Thursday, Davy is 'twitching', which we think is good, he's trying to wake up – Marion thinks differently – the twitching is a bad sign. Attempts at weaning him off ventilator and drugs don't work, so they decide to leave things for 24 hours and try again. Brain scan on Friday – 'Good' Friday' – confirms swelling on brain, causing twitching and they warn that even if he regains consciousness, there may be damage.

The immediate family is gathered to hear and face the results of the brain stem tests. *'There is no brain activity. Davy (your son, husband, brother, brother-in-law) is brain dead.'* The result and truth is too hard to take in, as Davy is warm to the touch and he's still Davy – just wake him up, he'll be okay.

After eleven days of illness and a titanic struggle to hold on to life, there was no waking up for Davy. On the evening of 12 April, I said my last goodbye and left Nancy and the immediate family to be with Davy for the inevitable end. That inevitable end came at quarter to five in the morning of 13 April 1993. There were no words, no consolation, no explanation that could make any sense of 'Why?'

There was no waking of the dead. After a mammoth struggle to live, Marion went to Davy for him to finally and formally die. Her less than five-foot, now fragile frame, clung to Davy for a desperate last time. A living nightmare has no sense of reality and no sense of justice and fairness.

REM have a number one hit with 'Everybody Hurts', and to us, it became Davy's commemorative song. Nancy, Trisha and Jeanette stay with Marion on an alternating basis to offer sisterly support in what becomes hours, days and weeks of greatest need, once the shock gives way to reality. Davy will never return – his wardrobe, clothes, razor and toothbrush are superfluous and his scent, voice and touch are at best recorded in video or memories of the past, but never again to be present in the future. A double bed with a wee teddy bear is no substitute for the big 'teddy bear' and the pillow becomes a sponge for tears that never seem to cease to flow.

The funeral service is arranged in the same church which had been the scene of Davy and Marion's wedding, in which they declared love and faithfulness, 'till death do us part'. The church and the service overflows to the cemetery in Hurlford. As part of the funeral cortege it is difficult to get to the cemetery and the newly dug grave evokes personal but now painful memories of helping Dad at the new cemetery in Darvel. Getting to the graveside we scan the hill above and it appears as a forest of newly sprung mourners standing respectfully between the headstones all around. The forest contains a swathe of Scottish Power Ayrshire employees, who decide en masse they will attend and catch up with work later. Individual people are not really recognisable as cord members are called and we concentrate on putting Davy to rest as gently as possible.

Focusing on the task in hand with cord number six helps to stifle tears that flow all around and are only interrupted by the agonising cry of 'no' as the finality of the farewell/funeral is felt by father, mother, brothers, sisters, sisters and brothers-in-law, friends and other family. Marion holds it together but Don McLean's 'Bye, Bye, American Pie', a Davy favourite, is too much to contemplate.

We have photos of Davy but it's funny how it is some of the oddest possessions of Davy's which evoke the sharpest of memories and which are still capable of bringing a smile to our faces.

We have his old racing bike, a silver and now rust frame on tyres, which never seemed thick enough to take his frame.

We have a pair of his brown, steel toe-capped working boots, from his last job with Scottish Power.

We have £6 in a jar, which was his 'skin', from his previous job as a milk-boy.

We haven't the heart to throw the bits and bobs out and they remain like favourite ornaments which link you to another place and time and which, if lost or broken, would only be a source of further grief and sadness. We have 'treasured memories' of Davy. We have no Davy.

With Marion, there was little we could say as we had lived Davy's death with her. Being there for Marion became a rallying call and Nancy and Jeanette's weekend stays and meals with John and Trisha helped ease Marion through grieving and a return to work to the scene of Davy's death. Nowadays, this would have raised cries and the spectre of post traumatic shock and stress, but wee Marion was made of sterner stuff, which gave her the resilience which could not be discerned from her 'wee lassie' image and figure. Involvement became the key for Marion to 'get over her loss', but at the same time, it also became the focus to highlight her loss – at parties, meals, nights out, she was in company – on her own – nightmare was reality.

Painfully and slowly, some smiles returned to a cherub face and Marion joined us on holiday in Majorca. The sun, sand and sea have a therapeutic effect but music, in the shape of Don McLean or REM became songs of tears as dry eye looks to dry eye in recognition and blinks away, but fails to hide the tears that flow freely and unashamedly. Marion comes to stay with us on a more regular basis and Nancy, Jeanette and me enjoy a drink with her, before Nancy and Jeanette call it a day and go to bed, sometime in October 1994. I stay with Marion to 'have another wee drink', and I 'fuss' over her and how she's getting on. The response is, *'I'm no a wee lassie, I'm nearly thirty and I know that I have to move on – you (and other people) can't wrap me in cotton wool – remember, I work in a hospital.'* This was after a year on and I thought she's right. A new normality is restored to Marion's life as she starts to take charge of her life, as it's evident Marion looks and feels better. The second Christmas since Davy's death was understandably looking a helluva lot better than the first.

Presents were bought for Gary, Greg, Mum, Dad, Mavis, Harry, Marion, Jeanette, Trisha... and stored away till the Christmas tree could be put up. Works nights out were arranged and Marion would join her long time pal, Pauline and her colleagues for a 30th birthday celebration meal in Ayr, on 17 December 1994.

That relatively late-night/early morning call came calling. Nancy is answering the phone and I instinctively turn down the telly, as the conversation does not ring true – there are too many question and gaps in the conversation – something has happened. Is it Mum, Dad, Mavis, Harry or some of the kids who've had a fall or an accident?

It's Marion – she's collapsed at a club in Ayr and has been taken to Ayr Hospital. Maybe she's just had too much to drink on a good night out; maybe her drinks have been mixed or spiked; maybe she's had an 'E' or some drugs; maybe, maybe, maybe?! Nancy, Jeanette and Trisha, picking up Mavis and Harry en route, rush to the hospital to be by Marion's bedside and get first-hand medical reports to dispel the 'maybes'. In the early hours of the morning, Nancy confirms the facts – Marion's had a brain haemorrhage and it's touch and go. As early as is reasonable, I take Gary and Greg to my Mum and Dads' to explain the position – as ever, it's no problem, but their eyes tell a story of absolute concern and dismay.

On arrival at the hospital, Nancy updates me on the position and 'progress' to date. Naturally agitated, she explains that they have been waiting for over two hours for the doctor to come back and give the results of 'tests'. We attempt to go into the room to see Marion and the nurse firmly but politely confirms that we can't come in. Another twenty minutes elapse and we 'push' to get in after the nurse has disappeared to attend the next high-dependency casualty.

At either side of Marion, Nancy and I sit and try to take in Marion's calmness – there are no cuts, bruises or bandaging of the head – she is as she's been lately – quietly contented and warm with no sign of pain or anxiety in her life. I touch her cheek and she's warm, I press forward and say, *'Come on Marion, come on, wake up.'* We sit for a few minutes and comment on how calm she appears and if only the doctor would come, re-examine her and let us know how she would progress. From no sign of pain or anxiety, there was also no sign of breathing. Like a new-born Gary or Greg in their cots, we move forward to check for breathing – nothing. *'She's not breathing, she's stopped breathing,'* I try to say calmly and quietly, but cannot contain myself, and I rush to get a nurse. *'What's her name'* the nurse asks. We tell her. She repeats, *'Marion?' she repeats 'Marion?, Marion?, can you hear me?'* She checks for vital signs and says there are some and Marion is still living – after the huge unexplained delay, the family are asked in 'to be there' in what are now said to be Marion's last moments. Within two minutes, Marion is declared dead – perhaps this is a way to help the realisation and grieving process – at least we were there when Marion died? *'A subarachnoid haemorrhage is quite rare, especially in someone of Marion's age [twenty-nine]'* – I've heard this type of explanation all too recently and whilst true, it offers no real explanation of 'why?' We have what and how but the 'why' is never, ever answered and never will be. Harry, who's done pretty well to hold it together with a voluntary job at Crosshouse Hospital, sits holding Marion's hand and stares into her face and sings, 'A bonnie wee Jeanie McCall', over and over in a tormented state, which eventually he realises he's in, and makes way for other members of the family. A true maternal bond is broken along with the hearts of Nancy, Jeanette and Trisha, Marion's sisters.

Phone calls from hospitals that are the exact opposite of those made for newly born babies have to be made. I phone my Mum and Dad to tell them the news and see if they will look after Gary and Greg for a wee bit longer. The call starts out on a straight and factual basis and ends in uncontrollable sobbing – this time it's not Mum, but me, as she realises, for my sake and that of Gary and Greg, she needs to hold it together, despite all her own maternal instinct saying 'cry' – that would come later.

Ironically or symbolically, 'Stay Another Day' by East 17 is high in the 'charts' and it becomes our anthem for Marion. It is written in tribute and remembrance of another tragedy (the death of a brother) and the longing for him to be there – even if for just another day. The song, the anguish and emotions behind it are a painful but all too accurate fit that can still cradle a tear and hurt the heart. It may be naïve, even pretentious, to think and link the words to those that would do justice to a latter-day Burns' lament but they are real, relevant and irresistible in our memory of Marion.

> *'I touch your face while you are sleeping*
> *And hold your hand don't understand what's going on*
> *Baby if you've got to go away*
> *I don't think I can take the pain*
> *Won't you stay another day*
> *Oh don't leave me alone like this*
> *Don't say it's the final kiss*
> *Won't you stay another day'*

Even before Marion's death and the exact nature of it, with no nursing or consultant staff available or seemingly in attendance, the family were uncomfortable with the way in which Marion's care had been 'handled'. This became all the more intense with the death and the manner in which the consultant/doctor eventually explained what had happened. Scottish people are very slow in general to complain, especially in situations where essential services are stretched and trying to help, but in this case, the doctor's attitude and approach left Nancy with no option but to write a letter of complaint – it would not bring Marion back, but it might just make the doctor reflect on how he had handled this case and do it more humanely and respectfully the next time round? The letter was never acknowledged – let alone responded to!

Within two years of Davy's death, we were solemnly gathered in the same church where Marion and Davy were married and where Davy's funeral service had taken place. The Reverend Roy was becoming the equivalent to death and funerals as the Reverend Collins was to marriages.

'*She never got over Davy,*' was to be heard amongst the muffled cries in the church and at the cemetery, and I guess that's true, but heartache did not kill Marion – headache in the form of a subarachnoid haemorrhage did. We didn't understand it, we had never heard of it before, but then, few of us had heard of 'toxic shock' before. When Davie Cooper, the Rangers and Scotland football star died of the exact same condition, aged thirty-nine, whilst filming a football training video, and just a matter of months after Marion, recognition of what had happened became real – '*Our Marion died of that.*' Like many an illness, a brain haemorrhage was no respecter of age, talent, fame or age – it simply struck and left every family the poorer.

At the same 're-opened' grave as Davy had been interred some twenty-one months ago, Marion was now being committed to the earth. The cords were called out – Harry, John, Kenny, Faither Davy, Jim and Craig Clements, John Houston and Hugh Hewitson. Nancy, Trisha and Jeanette were there for her all the way, as we rested Marion alongside and reunited her with her Davy. The sense of loss was felt doubly acute as the injustice and unfairness of Davy at twenty-eight and Marion at twenty-nine, dying was incomprehensible. As we walked from room to room in Davy and Marion's house, it was clear Marion hadn't and never would have thrown out or given away all her memories of Davy, as we come across some of his clothing, records, CDs............ Every move, however slowly and delayed to clear the house for sale, became a trauma in itself.

'*Remember we helped decorate this room?*'

'*Remember this ornament? Davy loved it, but Marion hated it....*'

'*Everything is so neat and tidy...*'

'Remember the Picasso?'

Art had never been Marion's forte and when Jeanette went to the Isle of Man in 1979, Marion and Nancy had a room of their own for the first time (Marion didn't even go to wave her off at the harbour – she was too busy moving in her gear!) she declared she would like a picture for her room – how much would such a picture cost? Jeanette explained it depended on whether she wanted a Sara Moon or a Picasso.

'How much is a Sara Moon?'

'About £5/£10,' was the reply – a moment's hesitation to check her purse and Marion declares – *'Oh I'd better have a Picasso.'*

As they say, knowing the price of things is not really important; it's appreciating the value of what you have that counts and Marion had known the value of Davy, her Mum and Dad, sisters, relatives, friends and her job at Crosshouse Hospital.

Changes in life and death are also reflected by changes at work. In order to keep ahead or at least keep up on a professional basis, I decide to do an MSc in Human Resource Management at Stirling University. The deal is that Scottish Power will pay the course fee and I make up the time for my day release and if I fail, I pay the money back – no pressure? The course is modular with continual assessment of course work, an exam and a dissertation of some 15,000 to 20,000 words, involving a piece of work-based research. The day release is actually a half-day, extending into the evening, every Monday for the three terms. The course work and four assessments are completed and passed. Four down, two to go – I chose research into the increasing role and involvement of line management (Team Leaders) in HR activities, as the theme for my dissertation. My workload is heavy and the dissertation work falls behind and I am granted an extension until the 18th September to complete and submit my work. I contemplate 'chucking it' but know we can't 'afford' that, and I will persevere if I can find a way through it. Nancy finds the way – 'For the next four weekends, you are working to complete the dissertation.' It's agreed and I sit in my old office in Kilmarnock for the next four weekends to complete the task. On a few days, Gary and Greg join me and with videos in hand, we set them up in the Conference Room, which has an electronic drop-down 'picture screen' and a video projector. Crisps, sweeties and drinks keep them occupied for up to four hours, with the only interruptions being toilet breaks. The work is completed, typed and submitted by the revised deadline and all that is left now is to await the outcome of the exam and the grading of the dissertation.

With the excitement of school kids or undergraduates, I drive to Stirling for the 'posting' of the exam results. There's backslapping all round as pass after pass is noted – the dissertation grading remains the final hurdle to my MSc qualification. The result finally comes through and whilst not a distinction, it is a solid pass and I'm on my way to a third graduation. Depending on your perspective, I am in good company graduating from Stirling University, as in September 1995, Mel Gibson and a Braveheart contingent attend a special graduation ceremony. However, no disrespect to Mel Gibson, Jackie Stewart, Ian Bannen, Gavin Hastings, Catherine Zeta-Jones et al, I will have the best company at my graduation – Nancy and my Mum and Dad – no mistakes this time round – this will make up for 1981. My Mum is especially delighted and both are relatively fit to attend. Graduation day in February 1996 goes very smoothly and professionally. We meet and talk with fellow 'classmates' and eagerly await the ceremony. From school days onwards, it's a fairly familiar routine – sit in the specified order, await your call, row by row, and then proceed to the stage on the calling of your name, don't run and exit right. It's familiar to me, but absolutely unique to Nancy, Mum and Dad and that in turn makes it unique for me. The robes and the scroll don't quite sum up a year of effort, but the photo captures the absolute magic of the day in a way that words never will.

Maternal pride in me becomes maternal concern for Mavis (Nancy's Mum). She smoked years ago and has the equivalent of a smoker's cough, which is never really diagnosed as anything. A pain in the chest lingers and is not cleared by antibiotics (chest infections and variously angina, Meier's disease, gas leak are all suggested causes). Mavis is fifty-nine and pretty fit, but after a prolonged period of to-ing and fro-ing to the doctors and consultants, in November 1996 she is confirmed as not being as fit as we all thought – in fact she has cancer.

Looking back, it seems obvious, but then looking forward, nothing was obvious. Complications came at every turn as Mavis became diabetic in February 1997, (as a result of taking the steroids she was prescribed), then came the shattering confirmation that she had multiple lesions (tumours) in the brain, that are too far advanced to treat. At this stage, we begin to curse our luck and every no-use bastard that healthily walked the street; some of those bastards had our share of luck and there was no getting it back, so we got at them. Mavis' condition was terminal with the primary cancer being found in the lung, and the days, weeks, months, years question was answered by 'a few months'. Consultants and counsellors explained what was likely to happen and how it would affect Mavis, who was stoically resigned to her fate – she was stronger than us and more concerned for us than herself – but that's a mum.

Christmas 1996 was videoed in a new light and a huge black shadow – it would be Mavis' last – she knew it, we knew it, but for the kids' sake, no one could say it. It was a good, sad day and the kids got the biggest Christmas presents ever. Jeanette spent a huge amount of time with Mavis and it was emotionally draining, as Mavis became physically slower but so mentally alert, that her physical impairments were aggravated in her mind. Harry took a new focus on life or death, and made a fuss that Mavis didn't need or want. Social workers visited the home in Hurlford and given Mavis' condition, agreed that a stair lift would be vital to assist Mavis' failing movement and mobility. Harry, in a focussed effort to help and care for Mavis, was the first to try out the newly installed stair lift in the first week of February 1997 – Mavis watched in horror as the reality of her crippling fate came home to her.

Having been discharged from hospital on 29 November 1996, the how long question was getting to an acute stage and getting to us. How long became how short as Mavis was readmitted to hospital on 11 February 1997, and I visited Mavis in hospital on 13 February for the last time – Nancy was already there. Mavis was already on a high dosage of morphine when I arrived and when I entered, she appeared to be sleeping. On speaking to Nancy, Mavis opens her eyes and without hesitation, says, *'Hi Kenny, how are you?'* *'I'm............fine,'* and I'm struggling to cope with this and you ask me how I am? Typical Mavis. We talk a little and Mavis pulls at the needle inserted into a vein in the back of her hand and says, *'This is hellish;'* – that just about summed it up – this was hell and it was painful, even on morphine. The doctor is called and says she can't be feeling pain, as the morphine dosage is just about as high as they can legally give. This is hellish, but some 'adjustments' are made and Mavis seems easier in herself and drifts off, as I say my goodbye, to return home to Gary and Greg, leaving variously, Nancy, Trisha, Jeanette and Harry to see what the morning will bring. There was no miracle, only an ending of one pain, and the beginning of another, as we mourned Mavis' passing on the 14th of February 1997. Born on St Patrick's Day, 1936, married on 'D-Day', 6th June 1956, so I suppose it was fitting that she died on St Valentine's Day.

Even the Reverend McCulloch's faith seems to be tested by the news of Mavis' death, as we again gather in Hurlford Cemetery (Riccarton), some twenty-five feet from Marion and Davys' grave to bury Mavis. Again, the cords are called out, Harry, John, Kenny – but relatively unusual in Scotland,

Trisha, Nancy and Jeanette proudly take their mother's cords (Bob McEwan and Allan Connell take the remaining two). In a sense, Mavis' death was worse than Davy and Marions', as we all knew for longer what was happening, but still remained absolutely helpless, as Mavis coped better than we did. Harry was coping well; he had all too dutifully phoned relatives and friends with the news of Mavis' death and the funeral arrangements, when confirmed. He was the focus of great attention and enormous sympathy and he revelled in it. Nancy, as usual, was quick to see that Harry's expectation of help and assistance from his daughters in his sad plight could and would never be matched by the reality. When the reality dawned on Harry that Mavis' death did not secure him the permanent attention he demanded, he sought this security by reverting to type. The bottle brought a better world and 'new and old friends' were acquired and reacquired, as Harry splashed out in an effort to close his 'attention deficit'. He moved in his new circle of 'friends' and entered a final spiral of descent, in spite of 'get a grip of yourself' conversations with numerous members of the family, but the grip on reality had been loosened and lost years before.

In a sense, I had a pretty narrow focus on these 'tragedies' – the events seem to take on a momentum of their own, like a volcano erupting and being faced by a white hot lava flow, which appears to be removing everything in its wake. Eventually though lava, like emotions, cool and hard reality sets in. There is a new physical and emotional landscape in its place – there is a realisation that what we've just gone through does and did happen to others. Close to home there are many examples – my uncles; Jim, David, John and Tom, and aunts; Annie and Margaret. The wider perspective was that my Mum and Dad had experienced the same types of anguish and emotions we had endured in a four-year spell or hell and now they also suffered on our behalf, in support and sympathy.

The family soldiered on in the face of adversity, and life had to go on for the sake of the kids. The kids literally became bigger and bigger features in our lives. For Gary and Greg respectively at four years of age, it was off to Nursery School, then at five, to the wee (primary) school and on to the big school (Loudoun Academy) at around twelve years of age. Along the way, Cubs and Scouts were attended, swimming lessons were a must and for two or three years, they represented the Valley Vikings at roller hockey. In between times, we went fishing for rainbows at the fishery in Lanark; went bike runs; went to the cinema and all the other type of things that normal families do or hope to do. We visited Disneyworld in Florida, which is tremendous, but also energy sapping and involves flights which add or take away two days of your holiday.

We decided to try something new – a week's cruising in the Mediterranean and a week in Majorca. The Island Breeze is a four-star floating hotel, casino, cinema, sports complex, ballroom, hairdresser, shopping mall and much more (service is service with a smile but not a plastic smile, but of generous warmth and interest, especially with two relatively young kids, who can still be utterly cherubic and charming). There were visits to Malta, Messina, Naples, Corsica and Minorca which were relatively short and sharp, but gave a great flavour of each and every location. We included day trips and half-day trips to Rome, Pisa, Lisbon and Barcelona which all offered the opportunity to behold some European wonders of the world – the Vatican; the Leaning Tower of Pisa; the Nou Camp and, surprise, surprise, a little piece of Darvel. The plaque read, 'Barcelona A Sir Alexander Fleming', above a bust of Sir Alexander Fleming in the public park. It seems that the Union of Matadors in Barcelona were so impressed by properties of penicillin to cure the wounds inflicted by wounded bulls that they paid for the erection of the bust in his memory. There appears, however, to be no such memorial stone funded by the 'raging bulls!'

Lisbon is beautiful, polished and professional and even the street urchin who came to our table at a local bar put on a show – playing his flute. He dressed in raggedy clothes which were clearly too big for his slight frame and only the designer trainers aroused our suspicions. He played the flute and fluttered a few dance steps before offering us a can so that we could offer our appreciation of his playing and his apparent plight.

The scene was played out at every table around the street bars and we realised this is a modern Dickensian sketch.

We spied a female Fagin who followed the raggedy boy and was in her twenties - going on forty. She did the 'junkie shuffle' as her boy danced and delighted to feed her habit. She shuffled from left to right foot almost on the spot and her right hand was run up to the shoulder of her left side and returned to scratch at her left wrist only for her left arm to return the complement to her right arm. She shuffled from right to left foot and moved forward one or two feet. She pulled a packet of cigarettes from her loose fitting jacket pocket, lit it and drew in temporary solace.

The 'junkie shuffle' was repeated until her last three fags had gone up in smoke and her only hope then was the contents of the collecting can. The later day Oliver Twist performed and picked at people's heart strings but only to get to their pockets. The female Fagin beckoned for the boy to return to her in desperation, emptied the can and cursed the tourist's generosity or lack of it. The raggedy boy got to keep one hundred pesetas and got to return to the tables with his flute in fake reality. You name the city and the view will be different but the scene will be the same.

Barcelona has different memories. Pets were not our forte. Goldfish won at the 'shows ' in a plastic bag that dripped until you got your goldfish home to transfer to a glass jar or bowl died after two days of feeding them breadcrumbs. Progression for us was to two exotic tropical fish in a real bowl with coloured stones and an archway to swim under. Greg's exotic goldfish was called 'Fruit Salad' and Gary's black equivalent 'Blackjack'. They were fed on fish food from the pet shop not breadcrumbs. Regular cleaning of the bowl would help prolong the lives of the fish, or at least Fruit Salad's. Blackjack didn't appear to relish life in the newly cleaned bowl and started doing a Michael Jackson. He couldn't actually moonwalk but gradually but perceptibly he was turning white – maybe washing the bowl in mild disinfectant was not so great an idea after all?

Blackjack aged prematurely, turned grey, then white and then turned over in the bowl. Nancy feared the worse in telling a young Gary that his fish was dead. She breaks the news gently – Blackjack is poorly and a bit off colour – in fact he's deadly white, which is a distinctly bad sign for a black fish. Nancy starts to cry as she explains to Gary that Blackjack has died during the night and the youthfully mature Gary states – I know Mum, don't worry, he was only a fish.

We've left our latest pet – Thumper, a dwarf lop rabbit, at home in the safe keeping of our neighbours – the Lyons- the name should have been a clue to Thumper's fate whom we've had since he was six weeks old and was now going on six years – our greatest pet feat ever. On board the Island Breeze cruise ship after a beautiful day touring Barcelona the news via the mobile is stunning. Thumper had been attacked and killed by a MONGOOSE. Even in the east of Darvel there were no Mongooses. Brother in law John explains the mongoose had in fact been an escaped ferret, which did the natural thing for ferrets, and killed Thumper before John relieved the ferret of half of its tail with a spade in an effort to save the ailing Thumper.

Nancy and Jeanette have a good 'greet' – this is more than just a fish, this was the family rabbit. Gary and Greg are sad by the manner of Thumper's death but have really grown out of childish affection to youthful acceptance – that's life and death – miss you Thumper.

Each of these holidays and every one before, however short, were accompanied by a note from Mum and Dad to wish us safe journey, a good holiday and a safe return.

Invariable within the note a 'luck penny' was tucked away for us to spend The 'luck penny' was not a penny, it was always pounds, but even if it had been a penny, it was the genuine concern which was of more and lasting value from parents who were literally generous to a fault.

One such note which was tenderly handed over on 20 June 2003 contains £100 and reads;

To Nancy, Kenneth, Gary and Greg,

I trust you will have a safe and enjoyable holiday. A well deserved rest from work. Come home refreshed in health and strength to start all over again.

I trust you all travel in God's safe keeping.

From Mum and Dad.

The note was written on a small three inch times three inch card with a bluebell flower on the front of it and contained in the lilac envelop was the £100.

I probably have twenty such notes for breaks and holidays before getting married and another fifty or so since.

It's unbelievable to think that this was done for us all and covered birthdays, Christmas, short breaks and longer holidays (Mum and Dad are not religious; weddings, christenings and funerals are church occasions, normal Christian life is not). However, religiously they have shown tremendous devotion to both immediate and extended family. The money was what they could or perhaps couldn't afford, the love and devotion was something that you couldn't bank but you could 'bank on'.

Back home, we've taken out season tickets for Kilmarnock Football Club and attend as many home games as possible, as both Gary and Greg take to playing the game with Galston Boys Club, in their respective age groups. Gary is not a natural football player and started playing in goal, as he is quite tall. Greg is smaller and has more natural ability. Both stuck in and did well in their first year with the Club. At an Easter tournament in Blackpool, Gary decided being a goalie doesn't involve you very much and got a game outfield and there was no turning him back as he was turned into a full-back. Another year on and both picked up the merit trophies in their respective teams and this reflects the fact that both are team players who are full of commitment and effort.

Killie also fared pretty well under Alex Totten and Bobby Williamson and reached the final of the Scottish Cup at Ibrox, on the 24th of May 1997, Greg's 8th birthday. Late in the day, we decided to go and I secured three tickets. The first half is fairly uneventful and even, as both Killie and Falkirk failed to break down each other's defences. As the half-time reflection began, 'Happy Birthday to Greg Rodgers' is reflected up on the electronic scoreboard and I quickly pointed it out to Greg – he was well chuffed and his Aunt Jeanette had made the day, as Killie eventually secure a 1-0 victory.

The Ayrshire District Management Team is reassembled at the Park Suite on 1st May 1999 and it was a 12.30 p.m. start. We were in dangerous territory as Walter Russell was attending and the hospitality flowed and flowed. At 6.00 p.m. we adjourned to the Killie Club. Eventually I staggered home about 9.00 p.m., having forgotten to phone home. On 'sprachling' through the door, it was evident we have had a mini family gathering – perhaps it was a party. No such luck. I'm no longer in a party mood, as Nancy confirmed her Dad died earlier today and I couldn't be contacted. I sobered up and offered to 'go and help', but it was too late for help that night. The events leading to Harry's death became clearer in the morning and it was confirmed, he died of a heart attack at home. Nancy, Trisha and Jeanette's years of frustration and worry over Harry turned to genuine tears of sorrow at the death of their Dad. We were back at Mavis' graveside later that week and again some twenty-odd feet from Davy and Marion, as Harry joined Mavis.

3a Craigie Road, Hurlford, is now empty – no Marion, no Davy, no Mavis, no Harry – no need to keep the house which had been the home to Nancy, Trisha, Jeanette and Marion from childhood. It's another break with the past.

The future and the year 2000 hurtled through space towards us. A new Millennium was looming and it was tempting to think – *'Things can only get better'*.

Marion's last photo at the party night out on 18th December
1984 (Marion is on the right).

CHAPTER FIVE
Millennium Mayhem and Magic

The new millennium accentuated our thoughts that we are getting older. 40th birthday parties and Silver Wedding anniversaries were more our 'territory' now. Even if you attend an 18th or 21st birthday or a wedding, there is in your mind a sense of no real change, but then you remember you are there as an uncle or an aunt and not one of the 'gang'. Your youth is going or gone but is also growing round you in the shape of sons, daughters, nieces and nephews.

Nieces and nephews have sprung up all around, as Lilian and Duncan have four children (Shona, Roddy, Alasdair and Lorna); Jim and Jessie have Bobby, Claire, Jim and Lilian; Marlene and Mike – Lorraine; Elaine and Alistair – Kevin; Bobby and Linda – Paul and Stephen; Yvonne and Jimmy – Jim and Ian; Avril and Andy – Aidan and Vhairi. Counting Gary and Greg, Mum and Dad have nineteen grandchildren. The cycle of family life continued and expanded as families become families within and beyond as sixteen further offspring extend the roots and branches of a living family tree.

I am proud to be Aidan's godfather and the christening was a great day in Middleton, just outside the centre of Manchester. Avril, following teacher training, graduation and a placement at our old school (Darvel Junior Secondary) had secured a good position in a school in the Manchester area. Aidan was a fit and healthy two-year old whose world is opening up before him – he was at a stage in learning where phenomenal progress is made. But just as easily as lights can be switched on, they can also be switched off.

An active and attentive Aidan became awkward and alone. Initially, the signs were minimal but are magnified in the comparison with the progress of his peers. Visits to Mum and

Dad became harder for Avril and Andy as they realised they could not quite articulate that 'something's not right with Aidan'. Avril and Andy struggled for over twelve months to get a diagnosis and come to terms with it before they could tell Mum and Dad what in their heart of hearts they already knew, as Aidan became a statistic in the great MMR debate – and is diagnosed as having autism.

The reports we read confirm that autism in children under eight has increased ten-fold since 1988. British babies now receive six vaccine doses in a unified shot before they are eight weeks old. They will be the recipients of another twenty-two doses before they get to school. Some fifty years ago, the only needle jab was for smallpox. The debate over MMR vaccination or lack of it rages on and is not likely to be settled in the near future. In the meantime, unless unorthodox or 'unapproved' treatment and medicines are attempted, Aidan's future is clear – constant, unrelenting care for a growing child who cannot understand or communicate. Adults too suffer in silence but also in anguish as Yvonne has a cancer scare and eventually has to have corrective surgery. If ever there was a six letter word to put the fear of God in you it is cancer and if ever there was a five letter word to absolutely understate that fear it is scare.

In the midst of all the misery of our tragedies, there was the enjoyment of some silver and golden moments. Mum and Dad celebrated their Golden Wedding Anniversary at Seamill Hydro on 31 March 1998. A Golden Wedding Anniversary is an absolute treasure; a joy to behold and yet it's also muted in its celebration, as a goodly number of the good people who attended the original wedding are no longer with us. There's emphasis on the marriage, the missing and the memories. Anniversary presents were abundant but were almost incomprehensible to Mum and Dad, who are simply delighted and dignified in the devotion they have shown to each other and their family. Lilian and Duncan, Jim and Jessie and Elaine and Alistair had all celebrated over twenty-five years of marriage.

Perhaps in search of our Irish roots, we ventured with Mum and Dad to Dublin. Dublin is a versatile and vibrant city but as a city, it was too hectic for Mum and Dad, who would have been more relaxed in the more rural Southern Ireland.

At the other end of the spectrum, Graham and Elaine 'ran away' to Gretna to get married, after years of living with each other. Marlene got remarried to Mike Gibb. Mike is not a 'Bee Gee', more a 'wee G' – a wee Geordie, who was as proud as punch to marry Marlene on 22 May 1999. Mike, like Marlene, had been married before and following his separation from Linda, the three kids, Jonathan, Nicola and Rachel took to the maternal Marlene like an older sister. It was not easy for Mike to work abroad a lot with GEC/Alston and support his new found wife and family but 'things get better'. Only David and Colin remained unmarried in the family.

'Things can only get better' if people strive and commit to making them better. Shutting our eyes and minds to take the easy option or dull the pain is not a solution. In Scotland, there was already a sense of 'off with the old and on with the new', as the new Scottish Parliament had been finally opened in 1999, with Gary in attendance for the big day. Gary was captured on video and the event and potential seemed to capture a nation's ambition 'to be a nation again'. After a prorogation of 292 years, we Scots looked to the Scottish Parliament as a source of innovation and optimism. In reality, innovation and optimism appeared to be to the fore but governmental cronyism and constipation were never far behind. The jury was out as the Scottish Parliament reached the end of its first term on 27 March 2003. The May 2003 elections produced another 'Lab-Lib' pact as the Labour and Liberal Democrat MPs formed a Government

However, the old Millennium was not quite out when the approach of the new Millennium conjured up ideas of renewing the spirit of a Darvel in decay. In marketing terms –

or estate agent speak – Darvel was the gateway to Ayrshire; the birthplace of Sir Alexander Fleming; a Lace Town, full of country properties at affordable prices and a warm and inviting community. Not all of this was bullshit and in best advertising parlance some of it was actually true, but the warm and inviting embers on the community fire were all but out. A few characters and a few clubs kept up the good fight to put the community back in Darvel – but it was an unequal struggle, against apathy, alcohol and amphetamines. It was also a struggle that virtually every other town in Scotland faces as personal commitment and endeavour replace social conscience and consciousness.

Ironically, it was mostly 'interlopers', those not born or bred in Darvel, or relatively new to the town who took up the initiative to breath more life into it. The Millennium Association is formed and comprised – Nancy, Trisha and Jeanette (the triple-trouble McCulloch sisters), Bobbi (Trisha's sister-in-law), Alexis, Lorna, the two Maggies, Dugald, Michael and Bobby, the town's SNP Councillor.

The immediate aim was to arrange an event at the town 'Square' to celebrate Hogmanay/New Year in the old-fashioned way – gather at the Square with family and friends, share a drink, have a laugh and enjoy the 'crack'. There could be a whole series of events for young and old alike to help celebrate the new Millennium and rebuild a community spirit which had been sadly lacking for many years. This was a task which the Millennium Association relished and Nancy, Trisha and Jeanette could look forward to help create some happy memories in the future without ever forgetting the tragedies or those happy memories of the past.

From 9.00 p.m. on Hogmanay 1999, at the Town Square, the hum of the diesel generator was silenced by the strum of Maggie McRae and the Tattiehowkers. Some eight hundred residents braved the elements and gathered at the Square to mark the historic occasion, hoping the millennium bug wouldn't bite or byte! Gary and I had our St Andrew's

Ambulance Association First Aid certificates so we were Millennium Association Marshals/First-Aiders. The atmosphere was lively but light as whole families took to the streets to form and take some community spirit. The grant from the Lottery Commission (obtained with a lot of help from Maggie McRae) was money well secured and spent. The new Millennium was welcomed in as never before and the people of Darvel began to see themselves in a new light. 'Will we have this next year?' and 'What else are you going to do?' were the most asked questions.

Community events, including dances, discos, quiz nights, ceilidhs, talent contest, sponsored walks, river cleans and open air café days followed and a bit of Millennium Magic was created through sheer hard work and effort, with a good measure of planning and team work thrown in.

The Community Council eventually woke up to the fact that the Millennium Association was making a bigger impact in the community than they were.

A Darvel Improvement Group (DIG) was formed to capitalise on the renewed interest in taking the town forward. The Millennium Association was 're-invented' as The Social Committee (and latterly, Entertainment Committee) and a hierarchy of committees was structured. With a hierarchy of committees comes a hierarchy of people – however volunteers and initiative do not generally sit well with hierarchies!? Burns' 'For a' that and a' that' should be a salutary reminder of the folly of rank and pretence. The headaches of hierarchies were temporarily out of mind as a Gala Day to remember was held in August 2002.

The event was captured in all its glory by the Valley Advertiser, which reflects on 'Darvel's Glorious Gala Day...

> *What a great day it was! The sun shone, the crowds turned out in their hundreds (if not thousands), the procession was excellent, and the varied programmes of events at the Morton Park entertained young and old alike. Many ex-Darvelites returned to the town from far and wide, friendships were renewed, and there was an infectious atmosphere of*

enjoyment about the town. The community spirit was almost tangible. After months of organisation by various groups throughout the town it was excellent to see the whole plan fit together, and the bonus was that the weather was excellent also.

The parade assembled at Campbell Street at 12.30 p.m. and Councillor Bobby McDill presented certificates to the floats and individuals taking part, all of which were colourful and imaginative. As the procession followed its route through the town, led by parade marshall Albert Anderson, the streets of Darvel were thronged with appreciative spectators.

At the Morton Park, Max Flemmich, Chair of Darvel Community Council, welcomed everyone before handing over to Reid Ross, Chair of Darvel Improvement Group, to conduct the programme. Provost Jimmy Boyd of East Ayrshire Council then officially opened the Gala Day and his wife, Mrs Anna Boyd, JP, crowned the Gala Queen, Fallon Spencer (11 years old), who made a confident speech about Darvel and the honour her town had bestowed on her. The Gala Day Princesses who accompanied the Queen were Heather Brown, Rhonna Glynn and Heather King. The Lace Queen tradition of the dresses being made from material supplied by local factories was maintained. On this occasion the dresses were fashioned by Joan Rankin from fabric donated by John Aird & Co Ltd.

After the crowning ceremony a varied programme took place in the events arena including an excellent performance by Black Rock Pipe Bank from Troon, historical re-enactment scenes by the Swords of Dalriada group, a children's sports programme, a fiercely contested tug of war competition, and a duck race (with plastic ducks) from Ranaldcoup Road Bridge to the Rab's Pool.

The large marquee in the Park was busy all afternoon selling tea, coffee and snacks, the beer tent ran out of beer, and the various craft stalls, ice cream and chip vans, hot dog stalls literally all had a field day. Ongoing throughout the afternoon were activities like beat the goalie, archery, laser quest, mini quad bikes, bouncy castles and inflatables. Other stalls sold keepsakes, stained glass, handknitting, sweets, greetings cards, jam, candles, plants, bottles baking, pet food and toys. Demonstrations of woodworking, painting, mosaics, spinning and weaving were also popular.

A novel activity demonstrated at the Park was the traditional Darvel sport of quoiting. Quoits are cast iron hoops varying in weight *from 2 to 16 pounds, and the experts demonstrating this sport were lobbing the quoits 40 feet onto a square metre of clay.*

All people involved in the huge variety of events which made up this highly successful Gala Day deserve the highest praise for their efforts. Particular thanks (must go to Darvel) Community Council and to Darvel Improvement Group, and, above all, credit must be given to the overall Gala co-ordinator, Neil McKenna, whose energy and enthusiasm provided the driving force for this event.

The organising committees would like also to pay tribute to the following sponsors – Scottish Power, East Ayrshire Council, Moonweave Ltd, J H Donald Ltd, ABP Signs, Milligans Electrical, Westsound Radio, Kilmarnock Standard, Lowes Transport, Ged Cunningham, McDonald Transport and Articulate Logistics. Prize donors must be thanked sincerely – Seacat, Scottish Co-op, Kilmarnock FC, Guinness, Clydesdale Bank, Woolworths, Marks & Spencer, Odeon Cinema, Asda, Heather's Florist, Westsound Radio, Moscow Leisure Centre and B & Q Superstore.

A video of the whole Gala Day – procession, coronation, field events – has been made in colour) by Bobby and Margaret Young and will be on sale soon. It captures the enjoyment of the day, and is a 'must' for all lovers of the town, a happy souvenir of a wonderful day.

The emphasis was on the rebirth and regeneration of the community but this needed individual initiative and commitment to help to reinforce the fact that families make a community as a family of families. Special fund-raising events were also a great success and sufficient to provide the opportunity for Rachel McColl to visit Disneyland with her Mum and Dad, before her tragically-short life was wrestled from her by cancer. Graham and Elaine's own personal triumph was also turned to heartbreak, as Elaine's pregnancy ended in the stillbirth of Cara. To Graham and Elaine, the pain of 'losing and never having' was stronger than 'having and lost', but it was a 'call' that no one should be asked to make!

Some three years on, the efforts of the original Millennium Association volunteers have helped engender a new spirit within the town. The talent shows, tea dances, line dances, discos, Street cafes, ceilidhs and quiz nights have all been successful thanks to the original Millennium Association and the ever helpful Ronnie (Karaoke) King and Sandy and Lilian Mair. The challenge is now for others to pick up the cudgels and the workload. The opportunity is for DIG leading lights to lead the way.

More emphasis is needed on providing facilities for the youth of this town to help capture their imagination and involvement. The planned skate park would be a welcome addition if the red tape and bureaucracy could be skated over. The town's celebration of its 250th anniversary ends in 2003 and in paying tribute to the past Darvel must now pay attention to the future.

In the meantime, there is tension in the town reflecting an age and culture clash. The roller-bladers and skateboarders attempt their 180°s and grinds at the area surrounding the town's War Memorial. What is lost on those condemning this action is that this is not an act of vandalism or disrespect for the dead but due to a lack of facilities for the youthful living. The youthful dead of the two World Wars on the War Memorial would surely understand and respect that. People should remember that yesterday's different often becomes tomorrow's norm. As Jocko Weyland eloquently tried to explain in *The Answer is Never*:

> *'Outside the local grocery I was stopped for skating on the sidewalk. The man wants to know when my type is going to learn our lesson. Skating away I know the answer to his question is never.*
> *– Lowboy (C.R Stecyk 111), 1981*

> *'Twenty years later I'm still at it. I'm not entirely sure why, though I do have some theories. The primary one is that there is an inexpressible freedom in the act of skating and also in the culture of skateboarding. It has influenced and affected many of the choices I've made in my life, informing almost everything I've done. I'm under the spell of an athletic activity that lies at a unique junction of sport and art. **There are no coaches, no rules, no one telling you what to do. It is a solitary pursuit that engenders intense camaraderie.** There are no limits to what can be done or imagined except for the ones*

you impose on yourself, because skating is open-ended and always evolving. It can be done anywhere there is concrete, and reconfigures the public spaces of modern architecture, using constructed areas in imaginative ways that become second nature to the skater but are not understood by the non-practitioner. Skating is a narcotic that offers release and a negation of self that defies analysis. **Skating is different.**

'...There is so much concrete and wood in the world that riding a skateboard is possible almost anywhere.

'...Why skating has had such a profound effect on so many people might be because it is a kind of play that defies any practical purpose – that is, it's fun. ... At some point in the middle of the twentieth century, the apple cart broke off the front of some anonymous kid's homemade scooter and the skateboard was born. Skating has now progressed from these humble beginnings to Hawk's and Rowley's feats, and along the way, what began as a toy gained tens of millions of adherents, spawned magazines and would change our culture, influencing music, fashion, art and film.

'...Concrete has become humanity's natural habitat, and this is what skaters utilize in a way no other group does. Because of this appropriation of the physical world, skating is inherently in conflict with authority. This taboo aspect fuels a 'The more illegal they make it, the more attractive it becomes' mind-set and has spawned skating's trademark rebellious behavior and ethos that other segments of society have increasingly come to emulate over the last twenty-five years.'

Skateboarding is different, difficult and diverse. Its History goes back over forty years, but unlike the 'twist', or the 'Jive' it has not been accepted. Its not fashionable to be a skateboarder or skater, but then again skateboarding is not about fashion, its more about a way of life. Again as Jocko Weyland explains:

'...Being a skater means a life lived differently, in pursuit of something elusive. Skateboarding is misunderstood because it is outside the normal scheme of things. The rest of the world often watches, follows and imitates aspects of skating without really getting it. It is a singular activity with fluctuating and contradictory philosophies, a true *subculture that has resisted attempts at going mainstream. Skating isn't nice. It's ugly and beautiful at the same time, a physical activity that isn't really a sport but is definitely a way of life.*

'Skateboarding is about getting towed behind cars, about riding off of picnic tables and ollieing onto them, about the sound of wheels carving on tile and trucks barking on coping. It's slamming onto cement and getting purple hip contusions that stick to your pants for weeks, riding on rain-soaked sidewalks and arguing with old ladies and running from cops. It's breaking your arm and getting your ramp burned down by hostile nonbelievers. It's skating the pools of abandoned houses or riding a good spot in a gang-infested neighborhood. Its boards breaking and wheels falling off when you're doing twenty-five down a hill. It's getting eggs, rocks and bricks thrown at you while doing ollies off a sidewalk bump late at night, or putting Bondo on cracks in rails so they can be slid down. It's inventive and often obscure board graphics, a way of dressing, a way of acting, of being.

*'...This isn't a textbook; it is biased, prejudicial and discriminating, while also trying to be inclusive and wide-ranging. **It's about the allure of scummy backyard pools and off-limits full pipes, of marble ledges and triple sets of stairs, of practicing an activity that has never really been understood by a public that is unaware of the rich rewards and inexplicable pleasures that start with the simple act of rolling.***[3]

The Millennium occasion fuelled a sense of renewal, if not rebirth. The family took part in some 'global expansion' of their own. Elaine and Alistair visited George (Alistair's brother) in New Zealand, to experience the sights and sounds of the Southern Hemisphere. The new soldiers, Bobby and Jim, formed part of the Royal Highland Fusiliers and have tours of duty in Belfast, Bosnia and Germany. The equipment and weapons of warfare may have changed since Wee Jock's

---

[3] Footnote: Excerpts from Jocko Weyland, *The Answer is Never A Skateboarder's History of the World,* Century, London, 1997.

day at the Battle of the Somme, but whether it be Belgium, Belfast or Bosnia, it is still about 'man's inhumanity to man'.

Joanne, in an effort to help eradicate some suffering, joined the Volu International Workcamp's Association of Ghana and adventured to West Africa for five weeks to help build a school. The inoculations and effort were rewarded through the gratitude of a people who eke out an existence, which was a far cry from Joanne's relatively comfortable life at Uni. It was a small but significant step in helping restore 'man's humanity to man'.

On arrival in Accra, the dream of the Volu mission to build a school turned to reality for Joanne and her friend Claire. They would be helping to build a toilet block within the school complex and both had to sleep in the upper bunk beds, as the rats had had the first choice and were fairly settled in the lower one. These were 'big, sleekit and not-so-timorous beasties' and eventually, Joanne and Claire were rehoused to a rat-free dorm, in old Ayomah, a six-hour drive from Accra. In fairly typical African style, this six-hour drive was made in a 'mini-bus'. Passengers and luggage were fitted to fill a double-decker bus doubled up on each other in cramped contentment and amazement.

At the welcome ceremony, the volunteers were embraced as brothers and sisters who had been lost in other lands and who had now returned home to lend a willing hand. The work was hard and basic but involved 'using your head' on the two-mile journey on foot through the forest to transport sand and water to the 'building site'. The seemingly simple process of balancing a bucket of water on your head and walking with it was a source of great mirth to the locals as Joanne had one 'wet hair day' after another 'wet hair day'. The fruits of Joanne's labours were 'bananas' and a toilet block - but not just any toilet block – there would be eight toilets in each of the two blocks but only four in operation at one time so that the other four, when full, could be shut and the 'end products' could be used as fertiliser!

The jovial Joanne endeavoured to make friends with the reticent locals but both the work and locals were heavy going and suspicion and unease are hard to bridge. In a material world it was a lack of materials or 'wee Cynthia's shoes' that provided the breakthrough. Cynthia was about twelve years of age, a naturally inquisitive and curious child, who was nonetheless shy and hesitant in the company of white Europeans.

Joanne's eye for detail spies out that Cynthia's shoes, or what passed for shoes, were beyond repair. A quick visit to the local store and a pair of what could only be described as 'flip-flops' were offered to an unbelieving Cynthia. In the material world these were only BhS or M&S run-a-rounds, but in the third world, they were precious and practical possessions. The free and unsolicited manner of the giving (Scots are famed for their generosity) produced an unexpected but welcome response. From the day following the giving to the day of leaving, Cynthia's Mum brought Joanne and Claire bananas. Bananas were the natural commodity to express their thanks for a small gift – the rarer commodity was Joanne's natural desire to do and give something to someone who had so very little. Warm memories of the unexpected return of personal and practical philanthropy eradicated those of rodents and the human rats who cheat and fail nations. Those memories live with Joanne and make her think, *'The whole experience was brilliant, it really makes me realise just how lucky I am and I'll definitely do something like it again.'*

Global movement turned out to be two-way, as Lorraine and JD, her South African husband, decided to give living and working in Britain a go. Jan Daniels Van Aswegan (JD) was a police officer in South Africa, but not the burly, brutal type depicted in the abuse of blacks in Jo'berg and beyond. He is as cerebral as Lorraine is comical – a couple that would be hard to pair from the individuals they are. JD's interest in computers led to a job in Nottingham and then Bolton where Lorraine became a hairdresser to the stars, or at least some Premiership and First Division English footballers.

On the home front, Galston Boys Club decided to invade Belgium and Holland! The under-12s, 14s and 15s represented Scotland in Europe at the Easter Football Tournament in Eindhoven. It was a coach trip to the channel at Dover and by tunnel to Calais, before travelling through France and Holland. The long journey was eased by the comfort of the facilities at Molenheide Holiday Village in Belgium. The boys of the under-14s were 'shared out' by 'degree of difficulty' – Andy and Kate drew the short straw or straws in the shape of Big Gary, Gal, Colin, Ali and Midget. Davy and Jane were next 'worse off' with their David, Kris, Duns and Calum. And we had our Gary, Craig Boy, Kenny and Kerr; Robert, Mel and Drew joined Andy and Helen.

The fine weather set us up for a football finale to remember. A glorious weekend was completed as the under-14s won their age group and the under-12s and 15s were runners up. The experience was brilliantly captured in rhyming form by Alex Milligan, Chief Reporter of the local *Kilmarnock Standard*.

The Footie Tour

Bags and cases lie around
The Galston boys are Euro bound
Jim Trainer checks we're all inside
The troops are set for Molenheide

Soon Smithy's in his sleepy haven
And we'd only gone as far as Strathaven
No bottle opener, Jesus Christ
As Lorna breaks the Smirnoff Ice

Soon we're there and in our chalet
A bite to eat and then a swally
The lads were great, the weather well
And boy were there some tales to tell

Organiser Bobby G
Who also doubles as V.P.
Described by some as Super-Gub
The biggest bastard in the club

Poor Vanda, married to our Lex
For one night had to forego sex
The poor guy's dislocated shoulder
Stopped him getting close to hold her

Mrs Paton, my oh my
Thought the pavements rather high
But snake Hips Audrey found a pal
When 'Oo-Ah Baby' shouted Gal

A rose among the sweaty males
Was the Baywatch Babe, physio Gail
Who's healing hands and magic potions
Gave the lads some naughty notions

Chairman Ian went on a hike
And was almost knocked down by a bike
His immediate reaction was to yell
'Have you no got a fucking bell'

Shortlees Carol, no one could phase her
She forgot to pack her razor
Gave the referee a fright
When she wished on him a prickly shite

Nancy Rodgers caused a fuss
As she sat waiting on the bus

Took it out on husband Kenny
'Cause she thought he'd had one too many

Mary Gemmell likes her lager
Too much sometimes makes her stagger
When she hears the punters roar
Mary pipes up 'What's the score'

There's a big one, shouted Kate
It's long, it's thick and stands up straight
Help ma bob, she must be gassed
But no, she's spied a mobile mast

It all went well, the trip was fun
The 12s and 15s almost won
The 14s finished in first place
To put a smile on Andy's face

We're heading home with driver Joe
A thousand miles or so to go
Galston Boys Club, shout it loud
You played it well and did us proud

Back on home soil, Greg progressed to second year at Loudoun Academy, whilst Gary sat his Highers in fifth year. Greg was artistic and something of a 'free spirit', and became a 'Mosher' with a real talent on a skateboard, so much so that he used his initiative and wrote off to skateboard companies and suppliers to seek sponsorship for his favourite sport. Gary was more serious and had secured good Standard Grades (6 one's and 2 two's) and had a career in medicine in sight – preferably as a doctor. He 'keeps his hand in', as we enrolled on a nine-week (evening class) course to renew our First Aid certificates at Kilmarnock College. Gary had held his certificate since he was twelve and the exam on 20 November 2002 was a breeze for him, but I struggled a bit.

The first aid exam was conducted in groups of threes and fours, and we were last to go. As we sat and chatted away the time until our exam, the conversation almost inevitably turned to accidents and death. We talked of a car accident in which two local teenagers had been killed, and we talked of someone's workmate who had died at the age of forty-five I was forty-five and there had been a rumour one of my friends died during the week.

'Do you know the person's name or what he did or where he stayed?' I asked.

The response is, 'I didn't really know him that well, but he was a clinical psychologist and stayed in Lugar – I think his name was Colin, I think his name was Colin.'

The echo was still in my head, as I heard myself query –

'Colin McLaren?'

'Yes, that's him – he's dead!'

It's not the best preparation I've had for a first aid exam, but I don't suppose McLaren planned it that way when he went out to lay some paving stones in his garden at the weekend. The funeral was over before I had received the confirmation of death and a weird feeling of 'that could have been me – I was at school with him – he's my age' – all pervade the thinking. Others dying older or younger have a reason, however inexplicable and unacceptable, but here is one of my peers, just keeling over and dying, as if it's perfectly natural!

It's all a bit disconcerting and distracting to remember a real character with whom you have shared some of the most defining moments in your character and realise he's gone. In his early 20s, he'd gone to Huddersfield Polytechnic, rather than a Scottish University and then 'dropped out' to become a croupier in the casinos in Glasgow, where I met up with him again after a gap of four or five years. He worked in Swaziland and then returned to an executive position with Save the Children, where again in Musselburgh, our paths again crossed. A degree in psychology at a Scottish University followed, our addresses did not follow our career paths. He was a character on whom I had based the fledgling attempts to write a book about apartheid in South Africa. The book was based on a good idea (a white-inspired rebellion to end apartheid), but never quite got off the ground in the face of sound advice from my big sister, Marlene – 'Why don't you write a book about something you really know about?' There's a sense of 'I wish I had kept in touch' and of 'I wish I had written that book' – but then there's this book.

Being old (or relatively old) and enjoying the respect and company of the young (or relatively young) is both admirable and achievable – Guy Collins is testimony to that! A weekend in Dublin celebrating a fortieth birthday party (Guy was sixty-nine) was followed by 'a day at the races' to mark his seventieth birthday. The Marx Brothers would not have looked out of place as the entourage descended on the Brigodoon House Hotel for drinks and dinner, before descending on the Western House for the Ayr Gold Cup meeting in September 2001. The gentry at the Western House needn't have worried, as 'the boys' did themselves proud. The event was so successful that the 'Turf Accountants' (at least we left from the Turf Hotel in Darvel) again dined at the Brigodoon and from there, sprinted to the Western House for the first race on 21 September 2002. There was Guy, sons John and Hugh, son-in-law Derek, the McAllisters (Ian – ex-captain of Ayr United – James and Alex), Jack McKie; John D Big Scoobie, Sanny, Bobby, Morton, wee Jim and another ten or so betting cronies and drinking buddies. The rafters of the Western House are again ringing to the sound of Elvis and the latest tunes of the day. The professional and polite join the punters in song – it's a day to remember – pure dead brilliant!

Another day to remember was 26 September 2002, as we celebrated twenty-one years of marriage (and Jim and Jessie's twenty-seven years). It was a bit daunting to reflect on twenty-one years of marriage and Gary nearing sixteen, when he could have left the nest to go to university, work or marry! Colin, my brother, after some thirty-seven years of staying with my Mum and Dad, decided to leave their nest and set up on his own. The house in Darvel which he bought and moved to on 1 August 2002 is less than a mile from Mum and Dad, but in emotional terms, it was a million miles away. Only Davy now stayed with Mum and Dad and it had been a lifetime since there was only one offspring in the house. The lack of the companionship of Colin in the family home was confirmed and reflected in visits to see Mum and Dad.

As Mum reflected, 'I miss him terribly.'

She is quick to confirm that she missed us all when we left, but Colin was a permanent feature of the home, much as a real fire was once the focal point of a living room.

For Colin, the gaps in his home life took a lot of getting used to and he was drawn between his home and the family home that was once his. In the run up to Colin preparing to leave for his new house, in typical fashion Mum and Dad declared, 'There will be a wee something for all of you when we're gone, but Davy has to get the house.'

At work the old adage of 'things happen in threes' seemed as if it could be positively coming my way as I was promoted from Employee Relations Manager to Human Resources Manager for Scottish Power's Power Systems Business. It's a big business with over three thousand employees who work to provide a safe and reliable supply of electricity to some five million customers in Central and South West Scotland and in Cheshire, Merseyside and North Wales.

One up and another two good things on the way!!

Events did happen in threes; there was the Fuel Crisis in September 2000; the outbreak of Foot and Mouth and a bout of Industrial Action for the first time in thirty years.

Yes, things happened in threes and if the black plague had been going around I think I would have copped for that as well.

As the Human Resources Manager I was 'lucky enough' to deal with these three emergencies.

The Fuel Crisis, which resulted from the lorry drivers' action to prevent the supply of fuel to petrol stations required daily emergency meetings to ensure our essential service could be maintained.

The outbreak of Foot and Mouth, that restricted the effective operation of the Business as access to land to either erect or repair electrical apparatus and overhead lines was denied or restricted.

The first bout of Industrial Action in over thirty years during December 2001 and January 2002, which involved nearly 2000 industrial trade union members of the AEEU, GMB and T and G.

From a Business perspective the industrial action was treated like a storm and through a 'business as usual' approach, the storm died down and life and business relationships had to be picked back up and improved. Working relationships with the full time trade union officials (Danny, Jim, Michael and Alan), shop stewards and employees had been stretched and strained and were only restored through realisation of respective positions and the renewal of mutual respect.

It was also a situation that had all the potential for family strife. In the blue corner was yours truly as Human Resources Manager (and previously Employee Relations Manager) and in the red corner 'brother Colin', Craft Attendant and GMB member. At the Gavin Hamilton Sports Centre in Darvel, we trained twice a week together but there was no personal strain or pain; we simply recognised each other's personal positions and got on with it. Like many an industrial dispute, individual views and relationships are subsumed in what becomes the management and trade union collective consciousness or perhaps, more accurately, collective unconsciousness. To Mum and Dad there was never really a quandary – they continued to support both sons. It was not a matter of equivocation or sitting on the fence; it was a matter of pride in both sons – 'striking never really resolved anything but you have to stand up for what you believe in' – there is in a sense no right or wrong, only steps that have to be retraced, redrawn and renewed. Mum and Dad could therefore, without contradiction, sympathise with me, Nancy and the kids and in my loss of a family holiday abroad in October, but they could and did equally sympathise with Colin in his loss of pay over six days of industrial action.

Brothers even in adversity were easier in a sense to deal with than the 'conman'. A Sunday afternoon's visit reveals Mum and Dad have 'switched' to British Gas for their electricity supply. An all too flippant 'well that will put me and Colin out of a job' reveals just how vulnerable elderly people can be. A tea-time salesman came a' knocking and got a foot in the door; 'no' was not taken for an answer and all it took to solve the problem and get rid of the guy was a signature. The duly-signed papers were shown to me and there was no 'cooling off period'. Within five minutes the agreement was deemed to be null and void as British Gas, to their credit, accepted the explanation offered. There is no apparent harm or loss but the vulnerability of all elderly people is highlighted, none the least to them.

It's a scene and 'scheme' that will be repeated a thousand times over in a thousand different 'scams'. Trust and respect for the elderly or lack of it is not the preserve of callous youth - a few mature individual and corporate consciences need to be pricked.

'Off with the old and on with the new' is a recurring theme as I took delivery of my new company car. It was a Mercedes 220 CDI and at about £25 grand it's weird to think this car cost more than the house we lived in when we bought it some seventeen years ago. Is any car more valuable than a house? Is any car worth more than a home?

At work I learned that my Managing Director (John Menzies of Ayrshire District and Cambuslang Rugby Club fame) was to retire on 31 March 2003. A fifteen-year association was about to be broken and new working relationships formed. Our first acquaintance at Waterloo Street in Glasgow as part of the Glasgow Clyde Area seemed fresh in the memory despite numerous changes to District, Regional and Functional structures, as our professional careers cross and re-cross. If the zenith was Ayrshire District then the nadir was the bout of industrial action.

As we celebrated Christmas 2002 and enter the New Year of 2003, it was a very typical Scottish (and probably worldwide) approach, to reflect on what's been and what will be? The old adage of 'what's done's done' comes to the fore.

The pain, suffering and hurt of loves lost are summarised each year in the Kilmarnock Standard Intimations.

This is not the Robert Burns 'Kilmarnock Edition', but for each and every family 'in memoriam' it evokes painful but proud memories.

We are no different as the tenth anniversary of McCulloch/Clements memoriam reads:

> *Remembering today and everyday, our Mum, Patricia (Mavis), Moodie who died on 14th February 1997, also Dad, Harry, died 1st May 1999, sister Marion, died 18th December 1994, and brother-in-law Davy, died 13 April 1993.*
>
> *Always in our thoughts, forever in our hearts.*
>
> *With love from all the family.*

It's a memoriam repeated in a thousand versions of the Kilmarnock Standard but there is nothing standard about the personal circumstances, emotions and grieving that accompanies each small note.

Looking back can be instructive, insightful and enjoyable, but whilst memories live in the mind, we cannot live on memories. It's not a case of forgetting, but more remembering and appreciating that things and people change and move on. If there are 'five ages of man' then Mrs Brownlie represents the character and substance of my Mum and Dad's parents in the 90–100 years old bracket. Mum and Dad, at seventy-nine years of age, really represented the fourth age and, somewhat unbelievable, we, I suppose, represented the third age. In a sense, we represented the 'old' (and not so old), but the remaining two ages lay with the nineteen grandchildren of the family, including Gary and Greg, and indeed, the sixteen great-grandchildren of Mum and Dad (Rachael, Ross and Rebekha; Rory, Melissa Aaron and Bethan; Alan and Andrew; Teigan, Kyle, Aidan; Jack; Emma, Amanda and Elise).

With so many in the family, birthdays were always looming but 10 March and 20 May are unique – Mum and Dad were seventy-nine – nearly octogenarians. 31 March 2003 was Nancy's birthday (twenty-one again) and Mum and Dad's fifty-fifth wedding anniversary. It's a lifetime of marriage and real parenthood that raises the ordinary to the extraordinary. Extraordinary courage was also required as the dreaded early morning call from Yvonne, on Friday 11 April 2003, confirms another death in the family – Marlene's Mike has died.

At around 9.00 p.m. that evening, I summoned up the courage to phone Marlene and let her know how sorry we are and that we are thinking of her.

From her house in Rugby, Marlene, in a calm state of numbing shock, explained;

Mike hadn't been well since about Monday and had flu-like symptoms, a high temperature and a really sore head. He'd been to the doctor mid-week and was advised to continue taking paracetamol during the day and Neurofen at night for his headache. By Friday he wasn't really any better. The visiting doctor prescribed antibiotics after we had told him how Mike had been and how he felt. I got the antibiotics from the chemist and Mike took one about lunchtime and one about eight hours later. We were late going to bed at about 11.15 p.m. and Mike was still uncomfortable, so I rubbed his back and he was really hot. We didn't really sleep and at about 1.30 a.m., Mike said he couldn't sleep and had to get up; he slipped out of his side of the bed and I got out of my side and put my dressing gown on. I walked through to the living room and Mike was supporting himself at the unit but as I came through, he started to slump to the floor and his hands couldn't hold him up. I caught him under his arms and eased him to the floor. He wasn't breathing – I tried to resuscitate him – his mouth was hard to open – I opened his airways and did two breaths and then started thumping his chest. I phoned for an ambulance and the doctor talked me through the resuscitation and kept asking, 'is he breathing yet?' – but he wasn't.

The doorbell rang and I left Mike to let the ambulance men in. They tried resuscitation and then the electric cardiac arrest shock treatment. They put the pads on Mike and the screen showed a straight line and a blip and then a line. They tried again and then said it would be better if I would get dressed. I went to the bedroom to get changed and couldn't get back out while they were working on Mike – I don't know how long I was in there but when I got out, the ambulance man said, 'I'm sorry' – I said 'You're joking,' and he said, 'I'm sorry.'

A doctor had to be called to sign the death certificate and the police had to come, as it was a sudden death. The doctor who came was the same one who had seen Mike earlier in the day. He looked at me and looked away and looked at Mike on the floor. He bent over Mike and took a wee while to stand back up and then he wrote out some notes and signed the paperwork and handed it to the police and then he just left. It took the police a wee while to realise what he had written and when they did, all hell broke out with the police contacting the health authorities to make their report. The doctor had written SARS (Severe Acute Respiratory Syndrome) – he couldn't diagnose it when Mike was living but he could when he was dead.

Eventually, the police asked me if I wanted some time alone with Mike as they put him back on the bed – they said he could stay there for up to twelve hours. I spent about an hour with Mike.

Early in the morning, the same doctor came back to see me and gave me a prescription for sleeping tablets and advised me to take them – I said I wouldn't. He said he would leave the prescription anyway and if I didn't use it to tear it up. I said to him then I wasn't happy by the way he had treated Mike – he asked me why? I said because he hadn't admitted Mike to hospital with all the symptoms he had. He couldn't look me in the eye, and just said, 'In hindsight…..' and left.

Lorraine and JD and Denise are here with me – I don't believe it – I must have done something really bad for this to happen twice.

There will be a post mortem on Monday and they said something funny that the results should be available later on Monday but I've read it takes three days to test and get the results.

I'm tired now; I'll have to go and try to get some sleep. Thanks.

There were no histrionics at Mike's funeral, only genuine family tears, fears and magical memories as the curtains at the crematorium open and close to the strains of Mark Knofler's 'Northumberland Man'. It had only been about ten days since Mike had gone to Pennsylvania; now he was gone for good. It was also twelve years since Frank died in South Africa and Lorraine, as then, was there now for her Mum. The family and friends, like almost every family, started to draw together and put a protective and supportive cocoon round Marlene as a poor but genuine substitute for Mike's arms.

There are six suspected cases of SARS reported in the UK on 11 April 2003 – a fact that tells you nothing. There were as yet no reported deaths from SARS in the UK. There are those who would suspect medical 'cock-up' and those who might suggest 'establishment conspiracy' but neither theory nor reality can return what has been lost. Mike would have been fifty-one on D-Day (6 June 2003), and, coincidentally, the day I complete the 'final draft' of this book. The inquest decrees that Mike has died of a lung infection but lo and behold there is no mention of SARS!

Life and death as the opposite ends of the spectrum can really be regarded as 'closest together' and so it is with Graham and Elaine who attend Mike's funeral whilst harbouring fears and hopes of new life. Days after Mike's funeral, Elaine's confirmed pregnancy offers Graham and Elaine opportunity to ease the still-painful memory of Cara's stillbirth. The bitter-sweet taste and rhythm of life beats on – the same in principle but oh so different in person.

On 19 December 2003 there is a real birth as a four pounds fourteen ounces tiny bundle of trepidation brings enormous relief for Elaine and Graham. The wait to bring Mikayla home is over as her weight is sufficient to gain release from hospital and join her mum and dad at home.

Our Galston Boys Club under-17s team have also found a new lease of life in the Scottish Cup and after beating Leven Thistle, Douglas Lads, Strathaven Dynamo, St. Peters (Paisley) and Paisley United a place in the final is theirs if they can beat Port Glasgow in the semi final at Somerset Park in Ayr in the semi – final.

Port Glasgow are beaten two nil in a fast and furious encounter that sends the pulses racing in Galston and the valley beyond. Airdrie's Excelsior Stadium is the venue for the final on Sunday 23 May 2004. There is no dream win at the end of the road as Calderwood Blue Star from East Kilbride prove to have a touch more skill in key areas and deservedly win 2–1. However the match report reads what might have been:

> *'NO EQUALISER CAME'* – *The Valley boys gave their all in a pulsating Scottish Cup under-17s final held at Airdrie's Excelsior Stadium last Sunday, but just failed to lift the cup.*
>
> *Their opponents from East Kilbride may just have had the edge on skill but the sheer hard work and effort and commitment of the Galston players should have earned them the right to take the match into extra time.*
>
> *And had that happened there can be no doubt that they would have gone on to lift the trophy with their opponents struggling to match the Galston's side's fitness levels.* [*]

It was a great achievement but the boys were shattered – it should and could have been so much better – but that's football. The boys were shattered but they remembered to congratulate the winners and shake hands with them all and as hard as it hurt we clapped hands when they, not us, lifted the cup. For Bobby Gemmell, Andy Black and myself the feeling of misery and hopelessness was worse than when we played and lost in cup finals ourselves – no amount of shouting, coaxing and coaching could change the result. We know it's all over but it's about to start again as under-19s next season!

---

[*] Extract taken from, Alex Milligan, *The Kilmarnock Standard*, 27th May 2004

At work there is also a 'birth' – it's the birth of a new UK Group – wide Human Resources Function under the direction of the UK HR Director of the Year, Stephen Dunn. Putting in place this new function displaces and replaces the best HR team I had ever formed and worked with in our Business Partner and shared service centre model – like cars the new model will have a higher performance, better economy and be able to handle all the turns and twists of the UK Businesses. The old team, Willie (and his entire shared services team), Kenny B, Kath, Hilary, Jim F, Irene, Joe, Ian, Linsey, Karen, Pamela, Jim McC, Bill, Lorna, Jim M, Mike, Heather, Dave and the luckless Gavin all have to find their new way in the new HR world but it's now a normal part of working life and change. As in life there are trade, business and work cycles and if and when you fall off you just have to get back on again and keep peddling away.

The Power Systems Executive Team also has some new talent – joining 'Big Davy' the M.D. and the 'old guard' (me, Dave, Gordon and Steve) are Dorothy, Janet, Marion, Guy, David W and Paul. The challenge of continuous change at work begins again – never ends.

Scotland fail (again) to qualify for the European football Championships, so we content ourselves watching England and other teams of interest. The ex Celtic player, Henrik Larsson, is a player of interest, so we sit and watch Sweden vs. Bulgaria on Monday 14 June 2004 – Dad although not a Celtic supporter liked Larsson as a player and as a man – no pretensions or poncing – an extremely gifted professional and hard working team player.

The game flows but there is no scoring when at 8.25 p.m. the phone goes. It's Marlene and in a short, low tone she delivers an unexpected message which has been on the telephone horizon for probably two years. 'Kenny, you better come quick, it's Dad he's collapsed and it's not looking good.' Experiences and emotions flood back and Nancy knows the nature of the call if not the extent even before I relay the message to her. I change out of my shorts into a pair of jeans and grab the mobile and make my way to 44 Glen Crescent.

An ambulance and paramedic car greet my arrival – it's a scene you've passed many a time and now wish you were passing again. I always entered Mum and Dad's house by the back door (the tradesman's entrance) but this was blocked by Dad's collapse in the kitchen. You could sense people watching the to'ings and fro'ings of the medics and relatives – you could almost hear them saying in hushed tones, 'It's Bobby Rodgers.' It's Dad on the kitchen floor, flat out, head towards the cooker and feet towards the dining table; Mum is distraught and tries to explain how Dad had been sick and collapsed and she couldn't get him up on a chair. The medics have two 'lines' into Dad; the evidence of Dad's reliance on warferin – thinned blood is smattered on the green carpet. There is a pulse on the heart monitor but not strong – it's weak like Dad. Marlene comforts Mum; Jim is by our Dad's side holding his left hand and Dad holds Jim's hand with a firm grip on him but not on life. Davy and Elaine are there and we speak to Dad, loud and clear, 'Come on Dad, we're here for you, come on.' And Jim says the response is a firmer gripping of his hand. The medics work at pace and professionally but breathings a problem so a clear plastic tube is inserted to Dad's throat – his breathing is aided and he seems more restful but is wrestling with life. When he's stable enough Jim accompanies Dad in the ambulance and the emergency dash to the blue sound of the 'meee-maws' is on – thrilling as a child but chilling as an adult. I can't keep up with the ambulance as it zips through Darvel, Newmilns, Galston and Hurlford to Crosshouse Hospital – here we go again! Davy and I arrive at Accident and Emergency (A and E) – 'Mr Rodgers, ah… yes, straight through, I'll take you to the room and someone will speak to you.' Jim is already there, 'Dad is going to be lucky to make it,' we all silently think but worse still for Dad would be 'making it' and left paralysed or in a vegetative state with no quality of life and not worth living. No worries on the latter point as a tall female doctor explains, 'You know your Dad was really bad when he came in, we did all we could but your Dad died.'

It's about 9.20 pm – Sweden are going on to beat Bulgaria 5–0 and Henrik Larsson grabs a double – Dad liked Henrik Larsson.

Colin, Davy, Graham, myself and Jim look around at each other and there are tears rolling down every eye – there's no wailing or gnashing of teeth but then muffled cries let themselves go as we hug each other. There's an awkward silence that is broken by the medical assistant who offers to let us go and see Dad in a few minutes. We all go but before then the mobile phone will take the small but stunning message, 'Dad's dead' back to all those waiting in Darvel and beyond. I tell Marlene – she tells Mum – for once you can actually feel the anguish and pain Mum feels. Nancy next and the whole circle of tears is complete. We go to Dad – he's fought his last brave struggle – it's a struggle he didn't lose – he won over twenty-five years ago when he beat his first heart attack – he reached his personal goal of being eighty with Mum – he wasn't paralysed, bed ridden or a brain-dead burden – that's what we all said to each other to rationalise the sudden but not unexpected departure of Dad.

He'd left us but left us in peace after giving birth to eighty years of his life and hundreds and thousands more for the family and the future. He's warm, no real sign of the struggle in the kitchen, in the ambulance and finally in A and E. We all touch him and have our own private thoughts and discussions but we all say 'THANKS DAD'.

We return to the Rodgers room, a drunk rattles around outside oblivious to reason or respect. Mum, Marlene, Elaine and Yvonne (wee Elaine, Jimmy and Lesley) all arrive. Lilian is in Sandford, Bobby in Dumfries and Avril in Middleton but they all know by now that our Dad is gone.

The police arrive – it's 'normal' for a sudden death and Jim, as eldest son, goes with them to explain events and provide details of Dad. The medical assistant is great; he gives us some forms/booklets and coffee and with the coffee, conversation rather than crying returns.

'Dad's target was really to get to eighty;' 'He would have hated to be an invalid;' 'He told me and Jim that if he was ever on a life support machine to switch it off, he didn't actually think or mind if it was illegal;' 'He always said the way he wanted to go was out fishing and having a wee dram by the water's edge and then lights out.'

It's all true and even if he didn't quite get all he wanted, he got the bits that mattered – no slow, mind-numbing decay – a relatively quick death.

Mum, Marlene, Elaine, Yvonne, Jimmy and wee Elaine arrive and go to see Dad in the hospital room at the mortuary. Almost sixty years of being together is together no more and the physical pain of having eleven children bears no comparison to the love of losing Robert (Dad). Everybody has a final word with Dad in the hospital and the night wears on and we leave to gather again on Tuesday morning. I drive Jim back home and agree to help him with 'the arrangements!' 'The arrangements' – two impersonal words that suddenly turn hugely personal and involve all the family. Tuesday 15th June is a bugger of a day – Dad's gone but did he hear us calling on him; did he know we were there for him, for Mum? The arrangements aren't really that hard to make after Big Jimmy pulls us together and to action – 'you might want to phone an appointment to collect the death certificate and phone the undertaker,' he sympathetically guides us to a conclusion to reach an end for Dad. Jim and I pick up the death certificate at 3.48 p.m. – it gives Dad's personal details and reads:

Time of death Monday 14 June 2004, 9.13 p.m.

Cause of death	*1.*	*Heart 'attack'*
		Heart disease
	2.	*Old age*

'Old age' indeed – that was a bloody achievement to reach eighty; there's many a man and woman who would be happy to die of 'old age' – eighty was a 'good age' without the sentence of senility. Infancy is for the very young – old age infancy, being constantly cared for, changed and spoon fed would have been a living hell for Dad – leave this infancy stuff to the kids. Eighty was a good age for Dad.

For nearly thirty years Dad had worked at the Darvel Cemeteries (the old and the new) and for much of this time Jimmy Dykes and George Collins (the undertakers) had been 'customers' of Dad at the cemeteries with their funeral cars and cortege. Today, George Collins would visit to make arrangements for Dad as a 'customer'. We agreed Dad would be buried in a lair on the top plot behind the house that was our home for some thirty years. It's where we had run, skipped, played hide and seek in summer and played in Mrs Smith's (the waiting room) in winter and we all recalled those times and Dad playing us to sleep to the skirl of the bagpipes – Mull of Kintyre, Amazing Grace and even Z-Cars!!

George took the details down carefully and waited patiently as we made out the words for our 'notification of death'. It eventually read:

RODGERS.

Suddenly at Crosshouse Hospital on the 14th June 2004 Robert (Bobby) in his 81st year of Darvel. Dearly loved husband of Lilian Allan, much loved dad, father in law, papa, and great grandfather to all the family. Forever in our hearts.

It could have been a five-pager if we'd listed out the whole family from Lilian, Jim, Marlene, Elaine, Bobby, me, Yvonne, Davy, Colin, Avril and Graham and the sixteen grandchildren and nineteen great-grandchildren. After the arrangements were made, I drove to the new cemetery; a journey I have made on literally thousands of occasions as a young boy, youth, with just Nancy, and then later with Nancy, Gary and

Greg, but this was unique. I was going to see the best resting place for Dad. I stood at the top plot – the cemetery was a bloody disgrace, Dad would have kept it a hundred times better than this – there was barely a level plot to be seen, the grass was mangled not cut, the edges were mashed and yet the view over the valley was stunning – this would do our Dad and only two lairs away from Graham and Elaine's little Cara.

Flowers too beautiful for this sad occasion start to arrive and are followed by a spray of sympathy cards that eventually number over a hundred. Friends and relatives write words on the cards that are easier to write than to read for Mum – all are absolutely genuine and simultaneously soothe and strike at the senses and the sense of loss.

The coffin's picked and the lair's ready for a Friday burial, Friday 18 June 2004; 11.45 a.m. for the house, 12 noon at the church and 12.45 p.m. at the cemetery. The minister (Dr. Robertson) comes to see us and he learns a little about Dad, he's relatively new to Darvel but is sympathetic and attentive and offers up a prayer in the house for Dad.

'Dad would have wanted a piper' – we all come to the same final and fitting conclusions. Jim Richmond, near-neighbour, ex-marathon running partner and friend of Bobby and family is a bonnie piper. With a tear in his eye he agrees to get time off work and pipe the best his heavy heart will allow – at the entrance gate it will be 'Colin's Cattle'; 'The Rowan tree' at the graveside – Mum liked 'Rowantree' and 'When the Battle's over' as a final farewell.

Everyone's gone to see Dad in his suit at George's place in Newmilns – everyone but Avril as she won't be up till Thursday evening – and me. Everyone including Mum says she's glad she went – Dad was good – a slight wink in his eye and a glint of a smile on his face. The family have placed their final mementos in the coffin with and for Dad. Graham, a teddy bear for Cara and a hip flask which is inscribed 'with Graham's thoughts'. Colin, some money, a lottery ticket (or a copy of the real one) with the numbers 1 (number one Dad), 5 (May, his birth month), 14 (date of death), 20 (date of birth), 24 (year of birth) and 40 (2 x 40 = 80, his age) and an un-scratched scratch card – Dad liked the lottery and a gamble. Marlene, Elaine and Yvonne left mementos but not memories. I've not gone to see Dad at George's. I want to remember him warm – it's a bit daft but that's what's in my head but in my heart I need to go.

I go on Thursday evening myself, before Avril, Andy, Jimmy, Yvonne and Elaine arrive. I see Dad and he looks good and warm but I won't touch him – that's the compromise. I say 'Thanks Dad,' again, and 'don't worry, we'll look after Mum,' and I leave a $2^1/_2$" diameter bronze medal of a fisher catching a trout.

Friday 18 June is another bugger of a day or at least it starts that way – it rains. It rains until the funeral cars arrive and then it clears. The church is busy for 'Bobby' when we arrive and old family faces not seen frequently enough nod in sympathy and appreciation.

We sing the 'Lord's My Shepherd' (Psalm 23) and 'Amazing Grace'. They are sung proudly but not too loudly as snuffled cries are only partly stifled by song. We pray – is it ever too late to pray? The minister recounts Dad's and the family's life and Mum, softly but audible to the front pews, corrects him – 'We were married on 31 March 1948, not 13 March;' – Nancy's birthday is the 31 March. We follow Dad's coffin to the car, only a few people are really recognisable as we slowly walk up the aisle. Heads sorrowfully bowed when they really should be proudly and heavenly high. Eddie Wilson is recognisable, with a face of tears that reflect years of friendship and a loss sorely felt: he's immaculate (as usual) and as usual, he's with Georgena, almost inseparable – our hands touch as I walk by. We all get into the cars and rays of sunshine replace the showers of rain. It appears as if half the town and more are gathered about the Central Church at the Square – the Millennium Party seems a millennium away.

The cortege meanders it's way out of town and past the old manse, where Mr Collins used to stay. The road narrows and steepens till 'Hillcrest'.

'Hillcrest, Manse Brae', the cemetery is in sight and we enter through the rusty green double gates to the strains of 'Colin's Cattle'. The sound and strains of Jim on the bagpipes almost symbolises being Scottish – we huff and puff and we strive to be better and there is this end product and pride of a noise which is not beautiful to the ear but hauntingly hair-raising – it is no different today, it is a noise and for spirits to be lifted and drunk by and it is a noise to lift the spirits. We all get out at the top of the cemetery on the widest road and on the road to farms above Hillcrest, people are streaming back down the hill, not to be late for 'Bobby' – we delay going to the graveside so that they'll arrive on time even if they are late for the late Bobby Rodgers. The grave has been dug by a mechanical digger which has left it's mark on the tarmac; it's mark on the grass is a gouged-out square hole. I almost wish I had dug the grave myself, neat and evened out and squared off at the shoulders and the feet.

We've decided that all the immediate family will take a cord; Mum and Jim, number one; Lilian and Graham, number two; Marlene and Bobby, number three; Elaine and me, number four; Yvonne and Davy, number five; and Avril and Colin, number six – Mum actually stays at the foot of the graveside – the head of the grave is three steps too far for her today. From the strain of the pipes it's now the strain of the cords, as we gently lower Dad's coffin – it's deadly still and quiet, the air is as breathless as Dad and yet, as we lower, a small windmill two lairs away starts a ratchety turn and turns some more as if mimicking each lowering we make. We all look up and laugh in our eyes, if not in our hearts – DAD! As we drop the cords the windmill stops, as if to say, 'I'm safely down now.' The minister starts his oration as we all join hands in a circle of sisters and brothers in arms around the grave – a car alarm breaks the solemnity and the minister tries to raise his voice above the level of the car alarm. Others at the graveside are thinking the same and smiles break grim faces as if to say, 'typical Bobby'.

Friends and family step gingerly forward to pay their last respects and the coffin is offered up an array of parting tributes. Flowers, coins, Bobby and Jim's cap badges, the soldiers' ultimate tribute and words soft on the ear but hard on your heart. Rhoda, Dad's eldest sister, a bit frail but bright as a button, simply and sisterly says, 'Bye Robert.'

The flowers too beautiful for a grave arrive – a double heart from Mum; single hearts, 'Papa' on flowers, pillows, sprays, heathers and thistles, all provide a blanket of warmth over a six-foot hole. Jim Richmond literally blows his heart out in the last lament. We adjourn to the Masonic Hall for something to eat and drink – it's full, full of respect and the warmth of friendly faces gloomed by the day and glistened by the sun – it starts to rain a little, nature's tears for the man. We meet and re-meet relatives, aunts, uncles, nieces, nephews, cousins and half cousins we half know.

Rhoda and William and Peter are Dad's only remaining sister and brothers – Peter has not made it to the funeral. None of Mum's brothers and sisters remains. Eighty was a good age for Dad.

The Hardys, the Wilsons, the Kerrs, the Croziers, the Allans and the remaining Rodgers are there. William Kerr the coconut man from Gan is there – he was a frequent visitor to Mum and Dad and he'll be sixty soon and he's crying and laughing at the same time and each family member and friend regale each other with a story of Dad. We decided we'd tell our story in memory of Dad and we all added bits till it became a complete memory, a story or series of stories worth telling and worthy of the man. I spoke for about ten minutes, backed up by Jim, Bobby, Davy, Colin and Graham, in case I broke down. For ten minutes, Dad was in the hall, as everybody hung on mental pictures of days before death. The stories were worthy and humorous and include:

Two old women stand at the bus stop opposite the terminus and see dad coming along towards them on his way to the old cemetery and they ask, 'Are you the young man who's going to bury us? And Dad says 'naw, I only bury the deid yins!'

Another sunny day he meets Trisha Collins along the water lip (the path by the river Irvine) and as he's carrying a fishing rod she decides to ask him if it is a good day for fishing – 'Naw hen, I'm no fishing I just havny got a dug!'

At weddings and anniversaries he would say to Mum 'I want a £100 for that pocket and £100 for that pocket' and he would get it, and he was never happy until he had spent it all on family and friends.

Even when he was ill he still had a very sharp wit and sense of humour as the local nurse found out.

The nurse arrives at the house to do an annual assessment on Dad and they get on the subject of mobility and if he can get up the stairs okay. Dad jokingly says 'I've got a chair lift now' and the nurse says, 'That must be a great help,' to which Dad responds, 'Aye, it would be if I could remember to use it.'

However Dad was not always right.

One early evening he returned home from work after one or two pints and says to Graham, 'tell your Mum to get the pot on there's three rabbits out there in the field. Graham, you come with me and pick them up when I shoot them'. So they creep to the railings outside and Dad fires off two shots and Graham cries out 'did you get them, did you get them?' as Dad walks over, kicks over some dirt and mutters, 'BLOODY MOLEHILLS!'

At last, the bugger of a day grew better and people laughed their faces dry – that's how Dad would have wanted it and everybody having a drink on him – so they did. As Dad would have said, Why all the long faces, you would think someone had died! Day drew to night lightly and, friendships and families renewed, people began to drift away from death to return to 'normal' life at their homes. The younger ones and some of the not so young ones, Bobby, young Jim, Yvonne's Jim and Ian, Kevin, Davy, Colin, are intent on drowning a few sorrows – so they do and only occasionally one of them breaks down as the drink heightens the sense of grief and loss but its been a good day – Dad would have enjoyed himself.

Big families, small families and the family of mankind are all touched by the hand of death at sometime, but this was our moment, our day, our Dad.

Before the end of the day, Graham's been back to the cemetery; he's arranged the blanket of flowers that's not just a patchwork quilt thrown on a bed, it's an ordered tapestry of tiered floral tributes.

Funny, weird things happened at the cemetery and after that, our minds were teased with a sense and signs of the uncanny and the inexplicable.

Mum's washing machine packed in and came back to life the same week, Our laptop, some six months ago, had been diagnosed by a 'computer clinic' in Kilmarnock as 'terminally ill' – the hard drive worked but the TFT screen was irreparable and would have to be replaced with a new one. I'd been loathe to pay an estimated bill for £350 and Gary and Greg connected the laptop's hard drive to our old IBM screen and this did the trick. The other trick was that on Tuesday or Wednesday after Dad died, the TFT screen on the laptop sprung to life as if brand new – what had Gary done different – absolutely nothing! Dad wasn't into computers, he preferred outdoor pursuits or, at least, he did before. There is probably some explanation, but none that we can fathom. Big Jimmy wins £250 on the horses – now that's beyond explanation! Jessie wins £250 on the Irish Lottery – Dad liked the lottery, especially the Irish one. Coincidences probably, but they kinda make you think and maybe believe, believe that there is something out there, some place that will be at home with

Dad's humour, humility and humanity and somewhere where he'll be able to fish, play darts, have a hauf and a laugh and play the bagpipes again!

It's hard not to, but we dwell too much in a past that has been lived; the moment is gone, never to be recreated; savour it and move on. Moving on doesn't mean you don't remember or you don't care or care less with time, it means respect and having the courage to face hard days, bad days and make more good days than bad days for you and yours.

Saturday 19 June is a good day – we're off (me, Gary, John Hamilton and Alistair Smith) to pick up the Scottish Youth Football Association (SYFA) and Dunfermline Building Society's 'Team of the Year Award'.

Ian Caldwell and wee Jack Elliot bring club captain, Kriss Patterson up and we all attend the SYFA AGM and presentation of awards.

If we didn't quite deserve to win the Scottish Cup, we deserved this award – for Galston Boys Club, for the supporters, the sponsors and the under-17 boys themselves. The trophy sits proudly in our cabinet in the living room and for a couple of weeks, it is flanked by sympathy cards, but upwards and onwards, the cards are packed physically away, but the award remains – no-one can take that away.

Summer is a new season and sparks new and changing life. Gary has attended his 'prom', 'all dressed up to the nines', or more accurately, 'all kilted out'. We dwell too much in the past. Our photos of Gary come back from the developer and there it is, it is the last photo of Dad alive. He's smiling with Mum and Gary in his kilt between them. Round every corner of your mind and walk of life you bump into your past but it is a past with renewed and refreshed people and experiences.

Renewed and refreshed is what we really need now. We have the opportunity to be renewed and refreshed at the Loudoun Academy Prizegiving.

The programme reads:

Loudoun Academy
Prizegiving Ceremony
In the
Assembly Hall
7.00 p.m. Tuesday 22 June 2004

PROGRAMME

- *Fly me to the moon – Jazz Band – musical introduction*
- *Chair's remarks – Mrs E McLean – Depute Head Teacher*
- *There are worst things I could do – Arianna Crotch – vocal soloist*
- *Head Teacher's Address – Mr B R Johnston*
- *Rock and Roll Parry Queen – Andrew Sloan and Alistair Bell – vocal duet*
- *Presentation of Prizes – Mrs A Gemmel – Head Teacher, Fenwick PS*
- *Vote of Thanks – Gary Rodgers – Head Boy*
- *Closing Remarks*
- *Dancing in the Street – Jazz Band – Musical Conclusion*

Gary receives a prize for first in biology and the Vesuvius prize for sport – thirty years ago I received that award and was school sports champion but, as they say, 'the older you get the faster you were!' Gary speaks well and the audience laugh in all the right places and times. There's a further following in footsteps as Gary will commence his degree in Biomedical Sciences at Glasgow University in September 2004 and then do a degree in medicine to become a doctor. Mum always thought I'd be a doctor but I'm too squeamish and struggle to give blood every year.

Our holiday cruising round the Med is another opportunity to get refreshed and we take in Palma, Palermo (Sicily), Naples, Ajaccio (Corsica), Marseilles, Barcelona, back to Palma and out again to Civitavecchia (the port for Rome),

La Spezia (Italy), Villefranche (France), Sete (France) and Palamos (Spain) before flying back from Palma.

I remember Sete from 1978 and even after twenty-six years it looks pretty much the same along the canals. The significance of the gondola – like boats in the canals becomes clear as I read, 'From the stands set up along the quays of the Canal Royal during the Saint Louis festival, you can have a close up view of a spectacular combat known as the 'Joutes' [water-jousting].' The winners deserve their memorable nicknames. Follow the men in white, the knights of eternal August and follow the fishermen too in their Saint Pierre procession. In Sete there's always people in search of beauty, singing poets, groups of painters and sculptors... all we were in search of in Sete was a taxi to take us back to the port where the Thompson Spirit awaited.

Pompeii was a world away. Monte Carlo is a different world as Gary and I visit the Casino and shelter from an impromptu and unfashionable shower that soaks the fashionable rich and poor alike.

Marseilles is much better than I remember and has a skatepark where Greg unpacks his skateboard and skates in freedom and as an expression of himself. The 'parallel' in Barcelona is not a skatepark but film crews capture the young and not so young skaters and boarders in the afternoon sun.

As usual, before we went on holiday, Mum has a luck penny for us to pick up – a £100 and a note which singularly brings home the fact that Dad's gone.

To Nancy, Kenneth, Gary and Greg.

I trust you have a safe and enjoyable holiday. Travel in 'god's safe keeping'. Come home refreshed in health and strength.

Thank you for all you help.

With lots of love from Mum.

It has been said that:
When you lose your parents you lose your past.

When you lose your child you lose your future.

But:

When you lose a husband, a wife, a brother, sister or close friend you lose your sense of justice, reason and what's right.

Often there is no justification, no acceptable reason, no respect for God and no sense of ever being right or being made right in the future.

It is in most people a temporary loss, permanently held and only tempered by reason, respect, memories and time.

The cycle of life irrevocably turns.

It turns for Lilian and Duncan, their sons and daughters, Shona, Roddy, Lorna and Alisdair and their sons and daughters.

It turns for Jim and Jessie and their Clare, Lilian, Bobby and Jim (the soldier sons), and their young families.

It turns for Marlene, now back at home in Darvel, and for Lorraine and JD in Bolton.

It turns for Elaine, Alistair and Kevin.

It turns for Bobby, Linda, and their Paul and Steven in Dumfries where Rabbie Burns died.

It turns for me, Nancy, Gary and Greg; Gary going to University and Greg skateboarding towards his standard grade exams.

It turns for Yvonne and Jimmy, and their Jim and Iain in their new jobs, making their way in the world.

It turns for Davy, at home with Mum – without the love of her life but still with a life of love to give and get.

It turns for Colin and Leslie sharing homes and their lives.

It turns for Avril, Andy, and their Aidan and Vhari in Middleton on the edge of Manchester.

It turns for Graham and Elaine and the oh so precious Mikayla – the youngest born of the youngest born.

The cycle of life irrevocably turns for everyone, in the sure and certain knowledge that, 'Everybody Has to Cry Sometime'.

UNIVERSITY OF STIRLING
Special Supplement

Published jointly by the PUBLIC RELATIONS OFFICE and the GRADUATES' ASSOCIATION

A SOUVENIR OF A SPECIAL WEEK
for those who were there and those who were not

September 1995

▼ *The Director and film star MEL GIBSON makes his way from the MacRobert Arts Centre to Logie Lecture Theatre with colleagues*

▲ *Locals KIRSTY YOUNG of TV fame and KENNY LOGAN, the Scotland rugby player*

▲ *BLYTHE DUFF, star of STV's 'Taggart'*

University of Stirling special supplement, September 1995, covering *Braveheart* with Mel Gibson and graduates.

University of Stirling, February 1996. Mum, Dad, Nancy and myself at graduation on receipt of MSc in Human Resource Management.

Top: Gary, Greg and Friend at Loudoun Castle.
Bottom: Gary and Greg – ready for Loudoun Academy.

Top: Nancy and Jeanette leaning at the Leaning Tower of Pisa.
Bottom: 'Four coins in the Trevie Fountain' – Gary, Greg,
Nancy and Jeanette make a wish.

Top: The 'Goldengate' Bridge in Lisbon – Gary, Nancy, Greg and Jeanette.
Bottom: Killie win the Scottish Cup in 1996.

The skateboarders at Perth

Top: Skateboarders – Greg is bottom right, No. 73.
Bottom: The 'new soldiers' – Jim and Bobby Rodgers with a
proud dad Jim.

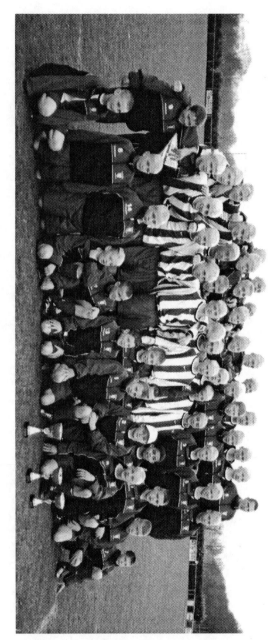

The victorious Galston Boys Club Under 12s, Under 14s and
Under 15s football teams in Belgium.

Top: Gary and Greg with their merit trophies.
Bottom: Gary going to the prom with Ariana and Natalie.

Top: A happy Mum and Dad at Jim Richmond's 21st birthday party, 2004.
Bottom: The last photo of Dad – Dad, Gary and Mum, 10th June 2004.

Galston Scottish Cup Finalist, 2004

Back Row: Kenny Rodgers (coach), Gary Rodgers, Stuart Melville, Kris Paterson (captain), Gary Denim, Craig Parker, John Hamilton, Colin Dunlop, Robert Gemmell, Bobby Gemmell (team manager).
Front Row: Matthew Richardson, Kenny Erskine, Craig McCaffrey, Alastair Smith, Drew Kirkland, Antony Gallagher, Andy Taylor, Craig Dunsmuir, Jamie Philipson.

Mikayla aged 8 months; 'the youngest born of the youngest born'.

MUSICAL EPILOGUE

The musical score to this book pretty much speaks for itself and reflects events and emotions to the full.

Elvis	*All Shook Up*	Infancy
Royal Scots Dragoon Guards	*Amazing Grace*	Hillcrest
Paul McCartney & Wings	*Mull of Kintyre*	Hillcrest
10cc	*I'm Not in Love*	Adolescence
Elton John	*Daniel*	Big Danny
Joan Armatrading	*Love & Devotion*	University
John Lennon	*Imagine*	University
David Bowie	*Life on Mars*	University
Sex Pistols	*We're So Pretty*	University
Whitney Houston	*The Greatest Love of All*	Gary
Tina Turner	*Simply the Best*	Greg
REM	*Everybody Hurts (Sometimes)*	Davy
East 17	*Stay Another Day*	Marion
Robbie Williams	*Angels*	Mavis
Ronan Keating	*If Tomorrow Never Comes*	Nancy
Frank Sinatra	*My Way*	*Determination*
U2	*It's a Beautiful Day*	Hope

There is no end.

'Happy is the man who can recall his fathers with joy, who with their deeds and greatness can regale a bearer, and with quiet pleasure beholds himself at the close of that fair succession.'

Goethe.

In memory of:

Big Danny; Davy Clements; Marion Clements; Patricia (Mavis) McCulloch; Harry McCulloch; Robert (Bobby) Rodgers and all the other friends and relatives we have lost along the way.